by Lane Wallace

Book design by Kimberly Sanders

Cover art and interior illustrations by Dennis Calaba

Book layout by David Faust
and Steve Lighthill

AVIATION FOUNDATION

Oshkosh, Wisconsin

© 2001 Lane E. Wallace
All rights reserved

Library of Congress Cataloging-in-Publication Data

Wallace, Lane E., 1961-
  Wild blue wonders : exploring the magic of flight / by Lane Wallace.
     p. cm.
  Summary: Explores the dynamics of flight and aircraft design, prepares the reader to begin creating original designs, and provides information about pilots and different types of planes.
    1. Aerodynamics—Juvenile literature. 2. Airplanes—Design and construction—Juvenile literature. 3. Flight—Juvenile literature. [1. Aerodynamics. 2. Airplanes—Design and construction. 3. Flight.]   I. Title.
 TL570 .W25 2001
 629.13—dc21

                                     2001032473

ISBN# 1-58932-002-6

Foreword

Where will the pilots and airplane designers of tomorrow come from? The answer to that one, of course, is pretty simple. They're walking among us today. We just don't know who they are yet - because right now they don't either. They're those hundreds of young boys and girls we see every day - fresh-faced kids who possess keen intelligence, boundless energy, and tons of imagination. Kids who are searching for that certain special "something" that will become their life's passion.

What we in the aviation community need to do is provide that special "something" - the spark that will ignite that passion - by explaining and showing our youngsters the wonders of flight and the opportunities it can offer in their lives.

That's why I'm so proud to be Honorary Chairman of EAA's Young Eagles Program, which every year - through the hard work of EAA volunteers - allows thousands of children to take that first airplane ride and experience the joys that flying provides. Through the Young Eagles Program, kids can not only develop a passion for aviation, but also learn that setting high goals as a young person is important, no matter what career they eventually choose.

Once you've got a child's attention, the key to piquing their curiosity is to "show them how it works" - which is what Lane Wallace's new book is all about. Lane is not only a gifted writer, but she also understands and appreciates the magical spell that flying casts upon the young. Wild Blue Wonders offers young people the tools and imagination they need to start turning those magical dreams into reality.

Chuck Yeager
General Charles E. Yeager
Honorary Chairman
EAA Young Eagles

**For every child who's ever run downhill,
arms outstretched,
and dreamed of taking flight**

TABLE OF CONTENTS

What Makes An Airplane Fly?

Flight 7
Our Atmosphere 10
Altitude & Aircraft 12
Forces Of Flight 14
What Makes Lift? 16
Lift In Flight 18
What Is Thrust? 20
What Is Drag? 22
Weight & Gravity 24
Flight Dynamics 26
Stability 28
Balance 30
Control 32

Designing An Airplane

Wings 36

Training Wings 38
Fast Wings 40
Long Range Wings 44
Short Take Off & Landing Wings 48
Airliner Wings 52
Cargo Wings 56
Aerobatic Wings 58
Flexible Wings 62
Space Wings 64
Helicopter Wings 68
Weird Wings 72

Control Surfaces 76

Variations On Control Surfaces 78
Cutting Edge Technology 82
Space Controls 86

Engines 90

Piston Engines 92
Jet Engines 96
Alternate Fuel Engines 100
Supersonic Engines 102
Rocket Engines 104

Landing Gear 108

Construction Materials 112

Supersonic Plane Design 116

Putting It All Together

Putting It Together 120
Put It Together Yourself 122
Design It Yourself 124

Fly!

The Cockpit 126
The Airliner Cockpit 128
The Fighter Cockpit 130
The Space Shuttle Cockpit 132
Flying Outside The Plane 134
The Sky's The Limit! 136

Wild Blue Wonders 138
Glossary of Terms 139
Glossary of Aircraft 144
Resource Guide 155
Acknowledgements 157
About The Author/EAA/NASA 158

Flight

Flight. Even the word sounds magical. Since the days of the cavemen, people have dreamed of achieving this magical feat. They watched the birds soar over the trees, imagining what it would be like to leave the heavy weight of the ground and take to the air. They dreamed of teasing the clouds, dancing on the wind, seeking adventure and tasting the freedom and the magic of the sky.

People kept dreaming about flight as the years and the centuries passed. Eventually, the myths and legends gave way to drawings of possible flying machines, models, and gliders. Leonardo da Vinci designed a possible flying machine in the 1500s. In 1783, two brothers in France finally built a balloon that could fly. And on a cold December day in 1903, two bicycle mechanics named Wilber and Orville Wright finally flew a frail wooden craft off the windswept dunes of "Kill Devil Hill" in Kitty Hawk, North Carolina. The powered flight of the "Wright Flyer" lasted only a few seconds. But it opened the door to a whole new world of adventure, exploration, and discovery.

In the span of a single lifetime since that winter morning in North Carolina, airplanes have gone from the Wright Flyer's 30 mile-per-hour speed to flying many times the speed of sound. Airplanes have also gone from flying those few hard-won feet above the sand dunes to flying 5 or 10 miles above the Earth. We've even figured out how to travel in space.

Once, designers didn't know how to build planes out of anything but wood, wire, and fabric. Now we build planes out of all sorts of exotic materials — titanium, Inconel X, graphite, fiberglass, and even mylar plastic. And if we want to, we can still build planes out of wood and fabric — but with far better fabric than the Wright brothers had.

From the simple straight wings of the early planes, we've learned to design planes with many different kinds of wings — angled, forward-swept, pivoting, short, long, thick, thin — and even flying machines with no wings at all!

The Wright brothers were doing well to have a plane fly in a straight line. Now we have planes that fly upside down, skyrocket up to 15,000 feet doing vertical rolls, perform spins and loops, hang motionless on their tails, and flip-flop in all sorts of unbelievable ways.

Yet we're still figuring out new ways to make planes fly faster, higher, slower, and better than we ever did before. There's always a better way to do something. And ideas that are only a dream today might be reality some day in the future if somebody believes in them enough.

We keep exploring new ways to design and build planes because we're still drawn to the sky, looking for new adventures within it the same way that sailors are drawn to the sea. Why is this? Why do we want to design planes that can fly or want to fly ourselves? Maybe because once you see the world from the cockpit of a plane, you never again see it quite the same way as people who have lived their lives Earthbound.

We've learned how to fly much better than we once did. But flight is still kind of magical, whether we're flying in an open-cockpit biplane or in a supersonic jet. It can take us places and let us do things people once only dreamed about doing. And the jobs aircraft can do are as unlimited as our ideas of what kind of planes we can build. Planes spray crops, rescue mountain climbers, carry medical supplies, transport passengers, fight battles, carry skydivers, take photographs and film movies, fly doctors into remote wilderness villages, and make the world a smaller place. They're also a lot of fun.

Looking at a plane taking off, it might truly seem like magic — this ability to defy gravity and lift into the air. But it's not. And once you understand what makes an airplane fly, it all starts to make sense. You can see why some planes have big wings, and others have small wings...Why some wings are swept backward and some are swept forward...Why some planes have jet engines, and others have propellers...Why some are made of fabric and some are made of metal.

Step into this world and see what makes these flying machines work. By the time you're done reading, you'll know so much about how planes fly that you'll be ready to draw and build your own designs! It's not magic. But it's still pretty amazing.

First, we'll show you what's really going on in the ocean of air that surrounds our planet, because that air is what allows airplanes to fly. Then we'll move on to the basics of what makes any airplane fly. (You can't figure out why a swept wing works if you don't know how a regular wing works.) Find out why you get squished into your seat at the bottom of a roller coaster or topple over to the side of the car as you go around a corner. See how skysurfers use their boards to maneuver around in the air. Take a closer look at why a NASCAR race car goes so fast, and how that relates to making an airplane fast.

After you have the basics down pat, you'll be ready to start designing a plane! Read on, and you'll learn how different wing shapes, control surfaces, engines, landing gear and materials change the kind of job a plane will do well. We'll also show you what some of those fancy dials and switches are in the cockpits of fighter planes, airliners, and the Space Shuttle!

We'll even give you suggestions on how you can go from being an outsider to being part of the flying community. You don't have to wait until you're 16 or 25. You can start now! But if you want all those airplane shapes and designs to make sense, you have to start at the beginning. And that means understanding the place where all those planes fly — the invisible ocean we call the atmosphere.

Our Atmosphere

The first step to understanding what makes airplanes fly, and why certain designs do some jobs better than others, is understanding the air in which airplanes fly.

The air above us may look like empty space. But it's not. Air is really a fluid, made up of billions of molecules that are constantly moving. In fact, if you could see the air, it would look just like a giant ocean surrounding the Earth, with waves, troughs, and constantly moving currents. When an airplane flies through the atmosphere, it's like a submarine moving through an ocean of air, with air flowing over all its surfaces.

A Look at Our Atmosphere

Just as the ocean changes as you go deeper, the atmosphere changes as you go higher. Near the surface of the Earth, the air is more dense, with many oxygen and nitrogen molecules in every cubic foot (a cubic foot is the air that would fill a box one foot wide, one foot long and one foot high). The number of molecules in the air decreases steadily as you go higher up in the atmosphere. Space is outside our atmosphere, so it has no "air" molecules.

The Earth's atmosphere has several layers. The one that affects us the most is called the **troposphere**. It goes from the surface of the Earth up as high as 40,000 feet (almost 7 miles!) and is the region where our weather occurs and where most airplanes fly. Air in the troposphere gets heated over some areas of the Earth and rises, while it cools and sinks in others. This causes air currents.

Near the surface of the Earth, moving air is also affected by the land over which it travels. Think about what happens when a river encounters large boulders or rocks that stick up into the current. The river tumbles over the rocks and boulders. The same thing happens with air. When it encounters a mountain or changing terrain, it has to flow over or around it,

Why does heat make air rise? Because heat makes air expand. This means there is more "space" in between the molecules, so a cubic foot of *hot* air weighs less than a cubic foot of *cold* air. This is why hot air balloons can fly. The heat from the burner makes the air inside the balloon expand, making it less dense and lighter than the air outside the balloon. As a result, the balloon rises.

which can cause turbulent, tumbling air currents.

Above the troposphere is the **stratosphere**. The stratosphere is a layer of very thin air (fewer air molecules) that's much more stable than the troposphere. Above the stratosphere is a layer called the **ionosphere**, where the molecules are electrically charged. Somewhere around 200 miles above the Earth, about as high as the Space Shuttle flies, the atmosphere gradually dissipates into what we call "space."

Effects of The Atmosphere

The fact that the atmosphere changes as you go higher has many different effects on both people and airplanes. If you've ever gone hiking on a mountain, you might have noticed that it gets harder to catch your breath up high. This is because the air has fewer oxygen and air molecules at higher altitudes. So your lungs are getting less oxygen with every breath. If it's hot outside, there will be even fewer molecules in the air, because hot air expands. This means that it's harder to catch your breath at 10,000 feet on a hot day than it is on a cold day.

When there are fewer molecules in the air, the air is less dense. This changes the amount of pressure the air exerts. If you've ever descended quickly in an airplane or car, your ears may have gotten "plugged." This is because the air you're descending into is more dense than the air you were in when you were higher up – and which is still inside your head. The denser outside air exerts more pressure on your eardrums because it wants to get into your head, where there is more room. By holding your nose and clearing your ears, you open up a passage so the air inside and outside your body can mix, making all the air the same density and pressure.

At extremes, these changes in pressure can be dangerous. When astronauts go into space, they have to be in a pressurized capsule or wear pressure suits. Otherwise, their bodies might explode as the higher pressure air inside their bodies tried to equalize with the extreme low pressure environment of space! Scuba divers who want to explore the deep ocean have the opposite problem — the water is *so* dense there that it could crush their bodies. So the team that found the Titanic, for example, used a pressurized submarine. And if you went scuba diving even 100 feet below the ocean surface, you'd have to wait 12-24 hours before flying at high altitudes, because your body might have trouble adjusting to such a big change in pressure.

Real Life Profile: Joyce Bowen
Balloon Pilot, Bonadventure Balloon Company, Napa, CA

Joyce Bowen knows a lot about how air behaves. She has to — she's a hot air balloon pilot. She uses different air currents at different altitudes to "steer" her balloons where she wants to go.

Think a balloon's too slow to be exciting? Fly with a pilot like Bowen. When she's not flying her balloons over the vineyards in California's wine country, she's doing things like competing in balloon races and flying her balloons across France and over the Alps in Switzerland. She was also the first person to fly a hot air balloon over the Mt. Pinatubo volcano in the Phillipines. She landed in a remote primitive village where she spent the day until her chase crew caught up with her. Now that's adventure!

How did she get to be a balloon pilot? By volunteering to work on the ground crew for another balloon pilot. "Balloon pilots are ALWAYS looking for ground crew help, so that's a great way to get into the sport," she says.

Altitude & Aircraft

In a sense, airplanes are just like people. They depend on air. They need air molecules flowing over their wings in order to create the "lift" that allows them to fly. And their engines need air to mix with the fuel in order for the fuel to burn.

Remember how a hiker on a mountain can have trouble getting enough air? An airplane at very high altitude has the same problem. An airplane engine needs air to "breathe," or operate. If there are fewer molecules in the air, there are fewer molecules to mix with the fuel. Fuel will only burn well in a certain proportional mix with air, so if there are fewer air molecules, it means the engine can't burn as much fuel. And THAT means the engine will develop less power.

Airplanes also need air flowing over their wings in order to fly. If the air is thinner, with fewer air molecules, the airplane won't create as much lift. (More on this can be found in the section on "Lift.")

What does this mean? For one thing, an airplane taking off at an airport up in the mountains where the air is thinner won't have as much power, and the air flowing over its wings won't be as effective. So it will take a lot longer for it to get off the ground. The overall performance of most small airplanes is worse at high altitude than it is closer to sea level. They won't climb as well or turn as quickly, all because the atmosphere has fewer air molecules in it.

Density Altitude

Remember how heat makes air expand, and therefore makes it less dense? (Think of how a hot air balloon works.) This can affect how an airplane flies, as well.

If it's a hot day, the air will be less dense, which means there will be fewer air molecules in each cubic foot. The air will *behave* just like the thinner air

Turbochargers and Superchargers

How do some planes produce enough power to fly at 20,000 feet if the air is so thin at high altitudes? They use special fan-like devices called **turbochargers** or **superchargers** to compress the air, squishing more air molecules together and making the air more dense, before it goes into the engine. This allows the engine to burn more fuel, which creates more power.

Even car engines use this technology for better performance. If you see a sports car with "turbo" lettering on the back, it means that the car uses a turbocharger to compress the air going into the engine so the engine can produce more power. (For more information on turbochargers, read the "Piston Engine" section.)

In order to find out more about the high atmosphere, NASA needed an airplane that could fly well at high altitudes, where the air is very thin. This unusual-looking plane is called the Pathfinder. It and a larger cousin, called the Centurion, are excellent high-altitude airplanes. They have very long, light wings and solar-powered engines so they can climb very high and stay there for a very long time. (Read the section on "Long-Range Wings" to find out more about these planes.)

that's normally found at a higher altitude. This means that on a hot day, an airplane taking off from an airport at an altitude of 2,000 feet may perform as poorly as if it's taking off from an airport at 7,000 feet.

Pilots would say this airport has a **density altitude** of 7,000 feet, because the hot air at the 2,000 foot elevation has the same *density* as air at 7,000 feet. A plane taking off from this hot airport will take a lot longer to get off the ground and will have more trouble climbing than it would on a cooler day. (Just like you would if you were hiking on a hot day.) This is important for pilots to remember because on a hot day, they might run out of runway before they get flying speed!

This problem is worse if a plane has a heavy load. The heavier an airplane is, the more lift and power it has to create to get off the ground. So on a hot day, when the air is thinner and creating less power and lift, a heavy airplane will take a LOT of runway to get off the ground.

Thinner Air = Faster Speed!

If an airplane performs more poorly in thin air, you'd think it would go slower at high altitudes, where the air is thin. But strangely enough, airplanes can go faster at high altitudes. This is because there are fewer air molecules present in the air there, so there is less resistance to the plane's movement. Because there are fewer air molecules the plane has to push through in thin air, it moves faster with less power. This is why race planes trying to set speed records like to make their attempts at high-altitude airports on hot days, when the air will be the very thin.

Forces Of Flight

NASA Photo

What Makes an Airplane Fly?

Even if it's not magic, it probably still seems amazing that something as heavy as a B-52 bomber or a Boeing 747 airliner can get off the ground. Ever wonder what makes this possible? The answer is, some very basic laws of physics. And these laws act exactly the same whether the plane is a little Piper Cub weighing 850 pounds or a giant four-engine jet weighing 250,000 pounds.

There are always four basic forces acting on an airplane in flight. These are:

1) **Lift,** which is the force "lifting" the airplane up in the air. In most cases, the majority of a plane's lift comes from its wings.

2) **Weight, or gravity,** which is the force pulling the airplane toward the Earth. The heavier the airplane, the greater this force is.

3) **Thrust**, which is the force propelling the airplane forward. In most cases, an airplane's thrust is created by its engine.

4) **Drag**, which is the force that works against the forward movement of the airplane. Drag can be caused by the shape of the airplane itself, or by the way the airplane's movement disturbs the air flow around it.

Real Life Profile: Jim Staley
Glider Pilot, Lake Elsinore, CA

Jim Staley always wanted to fly, but he didn't have the money for flying lessons. Then a friend's mom suggested he look into sailplane flying, which he could do at a younger age and which wouldn't cost as much.

Staley wandered in to the Lake Elsinore Glider Club and started hanging around, offering to help. Soon he was trading work for glider lessons. He worked during the summer hooking up tow ropes, running alongside the gliders to hold their wingtips until they got up enough speed to take off, and doing other tasks for the club. In return, he got his private glider license and free flight time.

Staley still wants to get his powered plane license. But he'll still keep soaring. "Initially I got into gliders because it was cheaper, but now it's a lot of fun and a sport for me," he says. "Powered planes focus more on getting somewhere. But they're both fun. Anytime I'm in the sky, I'm having fun."

How an airplane flies depends on how strong each of these four forces are at any given time. Lift does not always work exactly opposite to weight, and thrust does not always work directly opposite to drag. But all these forces are working in various combinations on a plane at all times.

Think of an airplane as suspended in air, being pulled in different directions by these four forces no matter what it's doing. How hard and in what direction the different forces are pulling will determine whether the airplane is moving faster, slowing down, climbing, descending, or maneuvering through the air. If you can picture that, you'll have the basic idea.

How do each of these forces work? It's not a mystery — it's a question of garden hoses, baseballs, balloons and bowling balls. Think we're crazy? Keep reading. It's true.

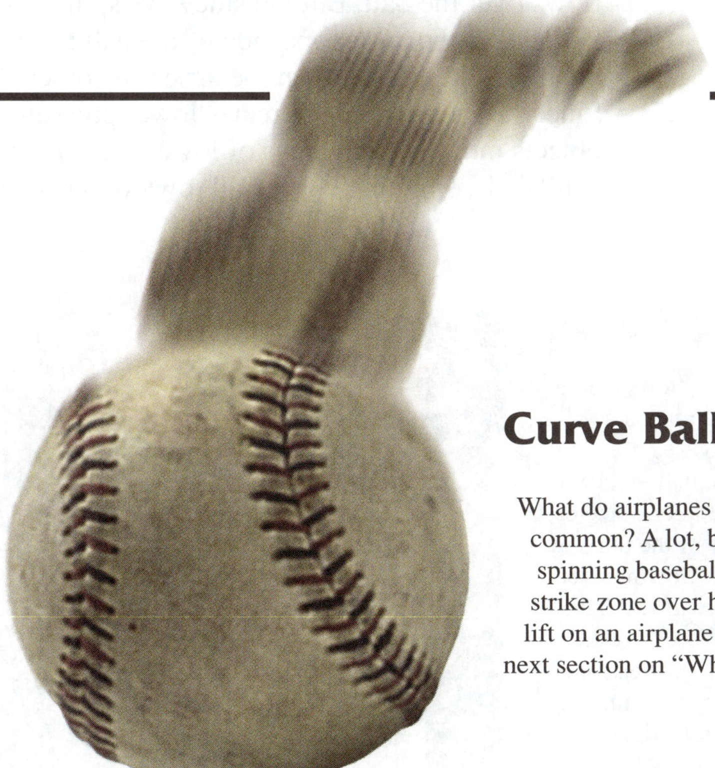

Curve Balls and Airplanes

What do airplanes and major league curve balls have in common? A lot, believe it or not. The forces that cause a spinning baseball to curve away from or toward the strike zone over home plate are the same ones that create lift on an airplane's wing. To see how this works, read the next section on "What Makes Lift."

What Makes Lift?

What is this mysterious thing called "lift?" To understand it, you have to remember that air is a fluid that flows, like water. Think about water flowing out of your garden hose. If you just leave the end of the hose open, it comes out in a thick stream right in front of the hose. But if you pinch the hose near its opening, restricting the amount of water that can come out of it, the water sprays way out ahead of the hose. The spray is thinner and moves faster than the unrestricted stream of water. The faster moving water also exerts less pressure on the hose. An easy way to remember this is to imagine two sides of a freeway – one side clogged in a traffic jam, and the other moving quickly. Which side appears to have less pressure? Right. The side with the fast-moving cars. The same holds true with water or air. Faster moving air or water has lower pressure than slow-moving air or water.

Bernoulli (memorize this and impress your friends!)

What really makes an airplane fly? The Bernoulli Principle! A Swiss mathematician named Daniel Bernoulli first figured out this "garden hose" theory about 250 years ago. He figured out that if the flow of air through a tube is restricted at any point, the air will flow faster and therefore create an area of lower pressure at that point.

It's also true that objects move toward areas of lower pressure. This is where the curve ball comes into play. A fast ball rotates top over bottom as it's thrown. But a curve ball spins horizontally, like the Earth rotating around the poles, as it moves toward the plate. As the baseball is thrown forward, air flows over the ball. But the sideways spin on a curve ball makes the air on one side of the ball move past the ball a little faster than the air on the other side. Since faster-moving air creates lower pressure, and objects move toward areas of lower pressure, this "pulls" the spinning curve ball toward that side.

Beach Balls and Ping Pong Balls

The same thing that causes a curve ball to curve allows a ping pong ball or beach ball to stay suspended over a fan (appliance stores or departments often show this kind of display to get customers' attention). The air from the fan keeps the ball in the air. But what keeps the ball from moving and falling off to one side or the other? If the ball starts to move toward one edge of the fan, the side of the ball no longer over the fan won't have air flowing over it anymore. But the part of the ball still over the fan will still have air flowing over it. The moving air will create lower pressure on the side still over the fan. Because objects move toward areas of lower pressure, the ball will be "pulled" back toward the center of the fan. (You can try this at home with a small fan and a ping-pong ball.)

Lift and Wings

So how do garden hoses and curve balls explain how an airplane flies? Picture a hose with a narrower section in it (as if you pinched a section between your fingers). The air (or water) going through this section will be moving faster, creating lower pressure.

Now imagine that the top half of that hose disappears. If you look closely, you'll see that the curved bottom part of the hose looks a lot like the curved upper surface of a wing.

Remember, air acts like a fluid that surrounds and flows past all the parts of an airplane. So the curved upper surface of a wing acts like a narrow section of a hose, restricting the flow of air going past it. This means the air going over the top of the wing speeds up, which creates lower air pressure on top of the wing than underneath the wing.

Since objects tend to move toward areas of lower pressure (like the curve ball), an airplane wing with air flowing past it will move up, toward the lower pressure above the wing. This is called "lift," and it's what makes airplanes able to fly.

The curve makes the air speed up

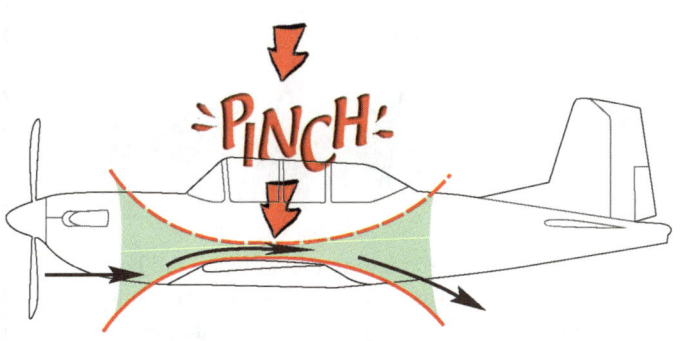

Try This!
An experiment with lift

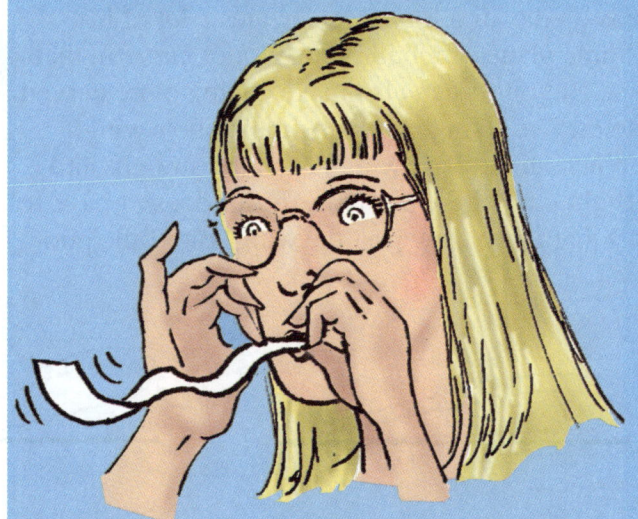

Want to see for yourself how moving air creates lift?

Step 1: Cut a strip of paper two inches wide by six inches long.

Step 2: Hold the strip of paper by one end and blow across the length of the strip on the top.

What happens? The end of the strip will rise up. This is because the moving air over the top of the paper strip creates a lower pressure area there than on the underside of the strip. Since objects move toward low pressure, the paper moves up, toward the low pressure. The same thing happens with an airplane wing.

Lift In Flight

Air flowing over a curved airplane wing creates *lift*. But the amount of lift a wing creates varies. If a plane is moving really fast, a lot of air is moving over its wing, which creates a lot of lift.

But when a plane is going slow, it has to create the same amount of lift with less air. To do this, it has to have a wing with a much bigger curve in it. Why? If the wing has a bigger curve, the air has to divert much further to get over the curve. This speeds up the air a lot, which creates a lot of lift.

Some planes are built with a lot of curve in their wings. But pilots can also make a wing more curved while they're flying by raising the plane's wing.

When an airplane wing is pointed straight into the flight path of the airplane, the air doesn't have to divert that far to flow past the wing. But if the pilot raises the angle of the wing so it's pointing *above* the plane's flight path, the air has to divert further to flow over the wing, which speeds up the air more and creates more lift.

In aeronautical terms, this angle between the airplane's wing and its flight path is called its **angle of attack**. The more a pilot *increases* the plane's **angle of attack** (the more the wings are raised *above* the plane's flight path), the more lift the wings will create.

By the same token, if a pilot lowers the wings *below* the plane's flight path, she or he will *decrease* how far the air has to divert to go around the wing. It's like taking the curve out of the wing altogether, which decreases lift and makes the plane descend.

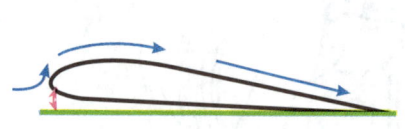

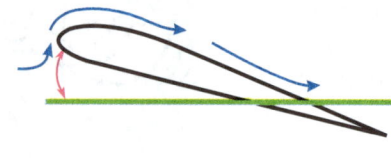

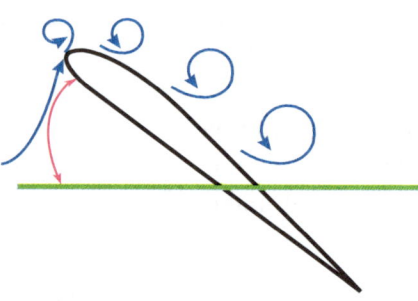

1. Low Angle of Attack. Here, the angle of the wing is only a little higher than the plane's flight path. So the air doesn't have to divert very far to get over the wing.

2. Higher Angle of Attack. Here the pilot has pulled the nose of the airplane up so that its wings are at a higher angle to the plane's flight path. That makes the air behave as if it's going around a wing with a much bigger curve in it.

3. Very High Angle of Attack, or Stalled. Here, the wing is at such a steep angle above the plane's flight path that the air can't get over it. If the air isn't flowing smoothly over a plane's wing, the wing "stalls," or stops creating lift.

Water-Skiing

In a way, water skiers are like airplanes. At high speeds, a water skier can skim along the surface with her skis nearly level. If she slows down, her skis will sit at more of an angle in the water (just like an airplane wing needing a bigger angle or curve at slow speeds). If water stops flowing past the skis altogether, she'll sink, just as a plane's wing will **stall** if air stops flowing past it (see below for more on "stalls").

Stalls

What happens if a pilot raises the wing's angle of attack really far? At some point, the angle is too big for the air to get around. When this happens, the wing is said to **stall**. The wing stops flying. But this doesn't mean the plane drops out of the sky. Planes are designed so that when the wing stops flying, the nose of the airplane drops. As soon as this happens, the wing's angle of attack becomes small again, and the wing starts to fly again.

Sometimes, however, pilots WANT to make the plane's wings stop flying. When? When they want to land. Watch a plane landing, and you'll see the pilot raise the nose of the plane right before it touches down. The pilot is raising the angle of attack of the wings gradually so that they will **stall** and stop flying just as the plane touches down.

Skysurfing

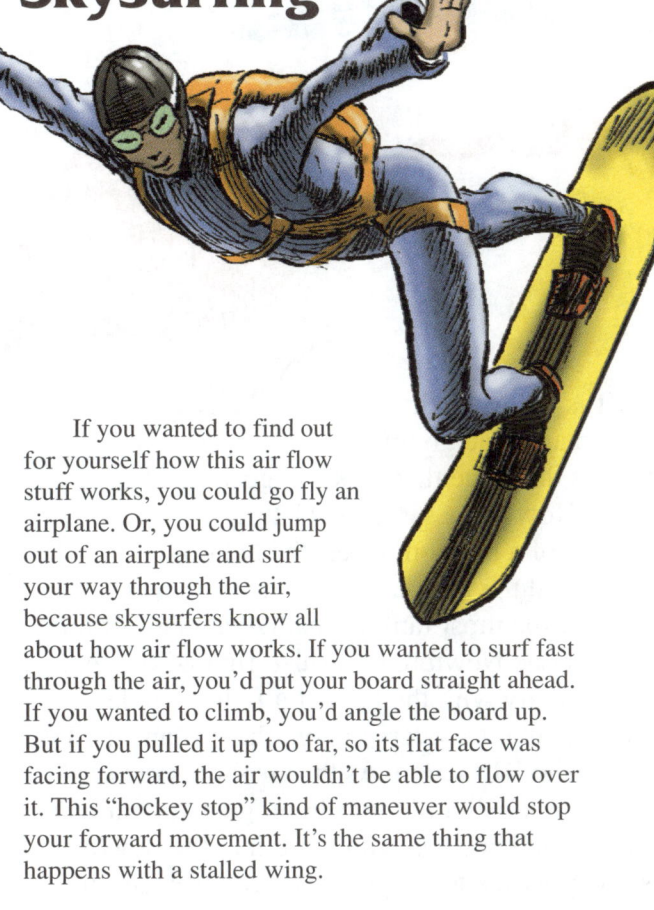

If you wanted to find out for yourself how this air flow stuff works, you could go fly an airplane. Or, you could jump out of an airplane and surf your way through the air, because skysurfers know all about how air flow works. If you wanted to surf fast through the air, you'd put your board straight ahead. If you wanted to climb, you'd angle the board up. But if you pulled it up too far, so its flat face was facing forward, the air wouldn't be able to flow over it. This "hockey stop" kind of maneuver would stop your forward movement. It's the same thing that happens with a stalled wing.

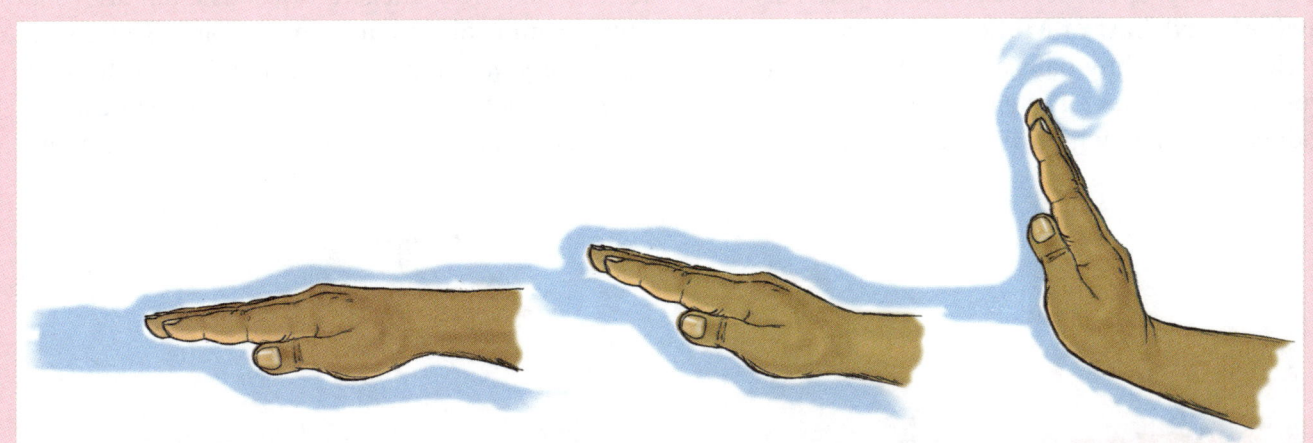

Do It Yourself Wind Tunnel

Want to see for yourself how **angle of attack** affects air flow? You can test it in your very own wind tunnel — the family car. Put your hand out the car window with your hand parallel to the ground, your thumb in front. Now slowly increase the angle of your hand so your thumb is pointed more toward the sky, while the car is still moving straight ahead. Feel how the air flow over your hand changes. Keep raising your hand from a level position up toward a vertical position. At some point, the air stops flowing over your hand at all. Your hand becomes a block to the wind, and you can feel how much the air resistance increases against your palm. The same thing happens as a pilot increases a wing's **angle of attack** enough to "stall" the wing.

What Is Thrust?

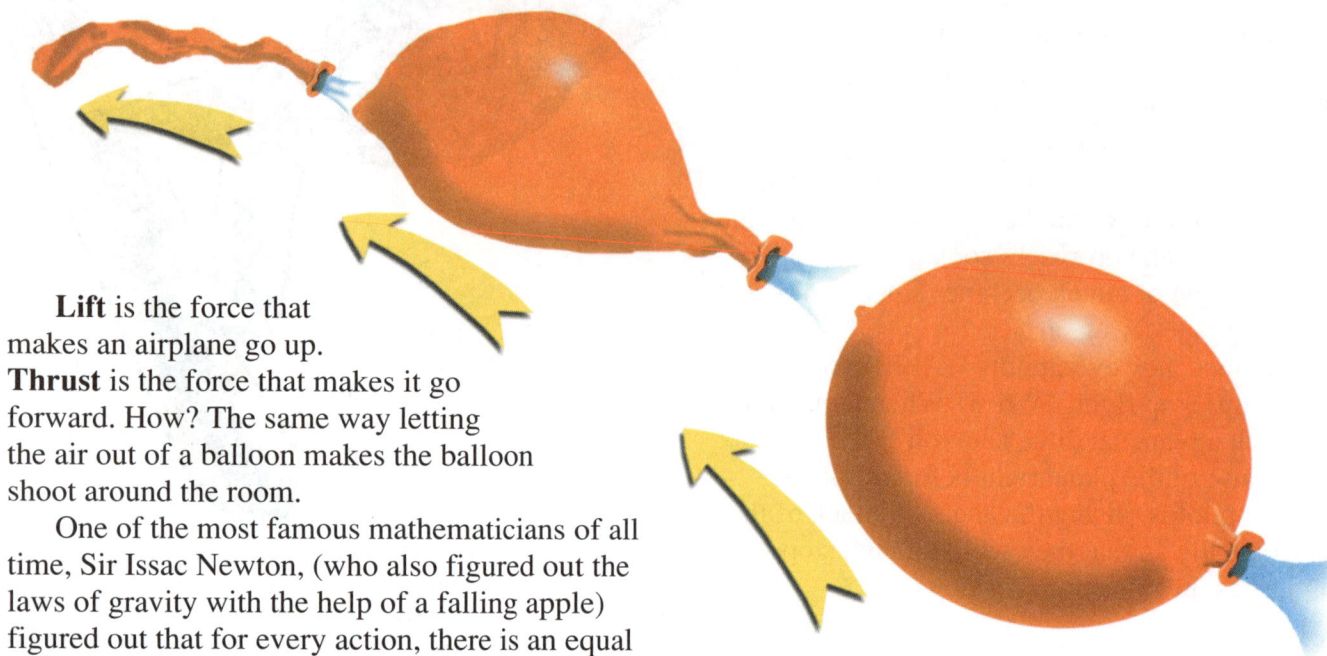

Lift is the force that makes an airplane go up. **Thrust** is the force that makes it go forward. How? The same way letting the air out of a balloon makes the balloon shoot around the room.

One of the most famous mathematicians of all time, Sir Issac Newton, (who also figured out the laws of gravity with the help of a falling apple) figured out that for every action, there is an equal and opposite RE-action. As the air shoots out of the back end of a balloon, the balloon goes forward. As a bowling ball crashes with force into the bowling pins, the pins scatter. If you're on rollerblades and you throw a football, the force of throwing the ball forward will propel you backward. Try it! This is **Newton's 3rd Law of Motion** in action!

How do bowling balls and rollerblades relate to thrust and airplanes? The engine of an airplane produces **thrust**, which is a force aimed *backward*, behind the airplane. The engine does this either by producing exhaust gases that shoot out the back of the engines (in a jet) or by running a propeller that drives air backward just as a fan drives air away from itself into a room. Because Newton's law says every *action* has an equal and opposite *reaction*, the backward force of the propeller or jet propels the airplane *forward* by the same amount.

Do-It-Yourself Thrust

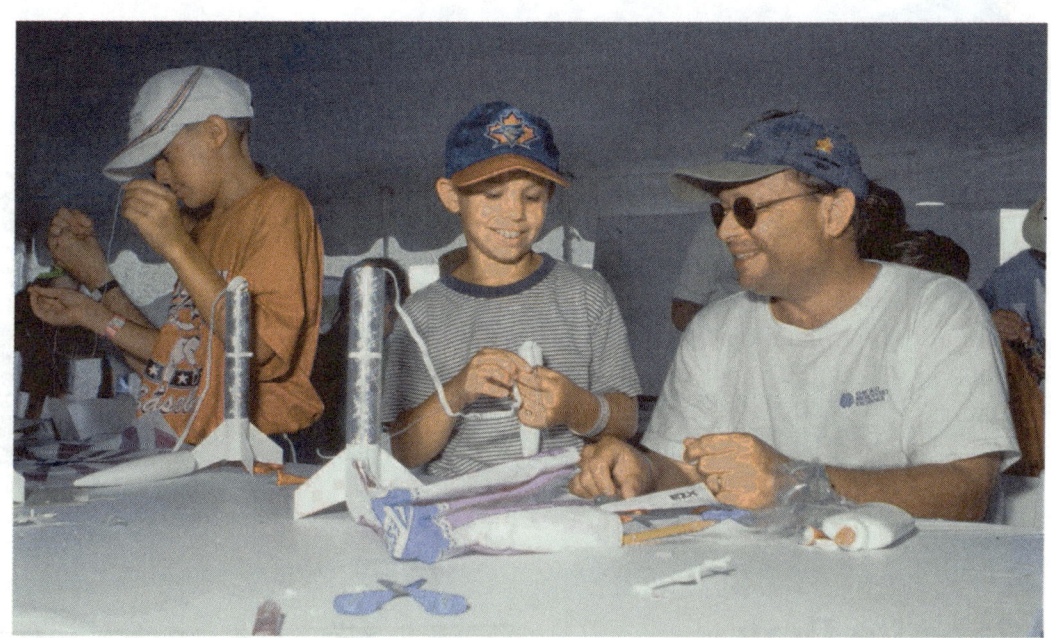

The young people in this photo are finding out how Newton's Third Law of Motion works by building their own rockets at the EAA Aviation Foundation's Air Academy summer camp (more information on the camp is on page 55). Rockets don't have any wings, so they rely entirely on thrust to fly. The explosion shoots out the back of the rocket, sending the rocket up in the air. Every *action* has an equal and opposite *reaction*.

Photos courtesy of EAA

No-Engine Aircraft

If engines create an airplane's thrust, how do airplanes without engines manage to fly? What creates a glider's thrust? The answer is gravity. For a glider to get forward speed, it dives. The force of gravity pulls it forward toward the ground, building up speed. When the glider, or sailplane, reaches an area where there is rising air, it circles, storing up potential speed in the form of extra altitude. When it gets enough altitude or slows down, the glider pilot points the nose of the glider down, letting gravity convert its altitude to forward speed once again.

What Is Drag?

You know what drag is. In most cases, anything that's a drag is something you want to get rid of. Homework, your little sister...anything that slows or drags you down. It's no different with airplanes. Drag is the stuff that keeps airplanes from moving forward. And generally, the more you can reduce it, the faster an airplane will fly.

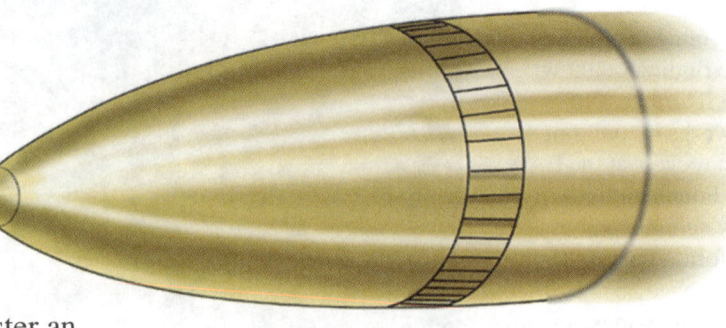

A bullet has very little drag.

A biplane has a lot of drag.

Parasite Drag

Drag comes in two flavors. One type is called "parasite" drag. It's named after the parasite bugs that attach themselves to other animals. Why? Because parasite drag is caused by things attached to the airplane. This includes wings, antennae, tail, landing gear — all the parts of the airplane that slow it down as it tries to plow its way through the molecules of air.

Some plane designs have a lot more drag than others. A shape that has very little drag is a bullet — it's why bullets were flying faster than the speed of sound long before airplanes were. But a bullet can't keep flying very long. It also can't turn or be controlled. So planes have to have some things attached to this basic shape to make them useful.

In the early days of flight, it was tough just to get an airplane to fly. Nobody worried about how much drag an airplane had. But as technology improved, designers began looking at how to reduce drag in order to make planes go faster.

The X-1

NASA Photo

Neat Fact

The speed of sound actually varies at different altitudes and temperatures. But at sea level, it's about 750 miles an hour.

Right after World War II, the Air Force and the National Advisory Committee for Aeronautics (NACA) — which evolved into today's NASA — decided to build an airplane to research flight at the speed of sound. The shape of this test airplane — named the X-1 — was basically the shape of a bullet with wings and tail attached. On October 14, 1947, Captain "Chuck" Yeager took the X-1 past the "sound barrier" for the very first time. (For more on the X-1, read the section on "Supersonic Flight.")

Induced Drag

The other type of drag is called **induced drag**. This is the drag caused by the movement of the airplane through the air. Drag your hand through a bowl full of water and notice the bumpy "wake" the movement of your hand causes. Or think of a power boat. As it moves through the water, a boat leaves a turbulent wake behind it.

An airplane does the same thing. As it moves through the fluid we call air, an airplane leaves a bumpy wake. The heavier and faster the airplane is, the bigger its wake will be. That bumpy air acts like a boat anchor, "dragging" behind the plane and slowing it down.

© Forest Johnson

Reducing Drag

If airplane designers want a plane to go fast, they need to reduce its drag as much as possible. How do they do this? Lots of ways. They can make the gear fold up into the airplane after take off or smooth the surface of the wings to let the air flow more easily over them. They can add curved fairings to let air flow over the plane more easily. Or they can add winglets (vertical tabs sticking up from the very ends of the wings), such as those found on newer airliners, to reduce some of the "wake" caused by the plane's movement. (To find out more about how these things work, and how to make a plane go really, super fast, read the sections on fast wings, airliner wings, and supersonic flight.)

But sometimes, believe it or not, pilots *want* drag. When they need a plane that can get down in a hurry without going really fast, designers may need to change a sleek plane design into a high-drag design. This is why dive bombers, fighter planes and many gliders have **spoilers** or **speed brakes** they can extend to suddenly cause a lot of drag and help the plane come down without building up too much speed. Most airplanes also have **flaps** they can extend from the wings when they're coming in for a landing.

With extremely fast airplanes, flaps may not be able to slow it down enough to land on a normal-length runway. These planes often have **drag chutes**, just like those used by drag race cars, to slow the airplane once it touches down on the runway. NASA's SR-71, for example, which is the fastest airplane in the world, needs to use a drag chute to slow it down when it lands. The Space Shuttle also uses a drag chute.

Drag and Cars

You can get an idea of how designers reduce the drag on airplane designs just by picturing the difference between a Ford Explorer and a NASCAR race car. The race car is designed to have as little drag as possible. It has smooth curves, very few sharp angles, and has what's called a "low profile," meaning it doesn't stick way up in the air. A sport utility vehicle, on the other hand, is designed to carry a lot. Its designers don't care if it's aerodynamic or fast. It has a lot of space inside, but it sticks way up in the air, has a lot of sharp corners, and a lot of stuff sticking out from it. Airplanes are the same way. Some are designed to carry a lot and are more boxy, and some are streamlined to make them fly very fast.

Weight & Gravity

In order to fly, an airplane has to overcome the force that keeps all of us pinned here to the planet instead of floating off into space somewhere. This force is what we call **gravity**. The force of gravity is what causes objects to have weight. Without gravity, none of us would weigh anything!

Airplanes are always affected by the force of gravity, even when they're in the air. If an airplane's engine stops working, the plane will still glide, because it has wings that will create some lift as long as the airplane is moving forward. But the plane will eventually come down, because gravity is pulling on it.

NASA Photo

Little Gravity = Little Weight

This photo of an astronaut leaping on the Moon shows clearly that if there were no gravity on the Earth, we wouldn't weigh anything. The gravity on the Moon is only 1/6 that of Earth. So the astronauts only weighed 1/6 of what they did at home. That meant that it took a lot less force for them to leap high off the ground, or shoot a golf ball way further than they could on the golf courses on Earth.

NASA Photo

The other important thing to remember about weight and gravity is that the more an airplane weighs, the more lift and thrust it will take to overcome the pull of gravity on that object. The NASA 747 that carries the Space Shuttle, for example, weighs almost three quarters of a million pounds — or about as much as 10,000 sixth graders — with the Shuttle on top. Talk about a heavy load! The Shuttle also creates a lot of parasite drag (think about the bullet versus the biplane), so it's really amazing the 747 manages to fly with the Shuttle on its back. (If you want to know how the airplane does this, read the section on Cargo Wings.)

Real Life Profile: Heather McRoberts
12 years old, Denver, CO

Heather McRoberts already knows she wants to be a scientist. But what McRoberts REALLY wants to be is a scientist in space.

She got to sample a little of what that future career might be like when she attended a week-long U.S. Space Camp in Mountain View, California. She got to train on the same kind of equipment astronauts use and got to try her hand at a "zero-G" wall that simulated what it's like to float and work in space. And a centrifuge machine let her experience the high gravity, or "G" forces, of lift-off. "At times you got squished into your seat, and other times you felt like you were floating, but it never made you feel sick," she reports.

McRoberts still wants to be an astronaut. In the meantime, she works on devising her own Earth-bound experiments. One of her latest was an attempt to grow stalagtites on her bathroom ceiling, using Epsom Salts. "Worked pretty well," she says with the satisfied smile of a true scientist.

Flight Dynamics

There are always four different forces acting on a plane when it's in flight. But how they combine to affect the plane changes, depending on what the plane is doing.

It's like a math equation that has to equal a total of 8. You can get that total by adding 2 + 2 + 2 + 2, in which case all the factors are equal. Or, you could have 3 + 1 + 2 + 2, or 1 + 4 + 2 + 1. The four forces act in different combinations, but the total is always the same.

How does this relate to an airplane? When an airplane is flying straight and level and is not speeding up or slowing down, all four forces — thrust, lift, weight and drag — are equal (2 + 2 + 2 + 2). But when an airplane is taking off, it's moving forward and up. This means that the forces of thrust and lift must be greater than the forces of weight and drag (3 + 3 + 1 + 1). If the plane is descending and slowing down, on the other hand, the forces of thrust and lift must be less than those of weight and drag (1 + 1 + 3 + 3).

If an airplane is in a turn, the numbers in the equation also change. This is because in a turn, the top side of the wings, which create most of the lift, aren't facing straight up. As a result, the plane's lift isn't pulling the plane straight up, but the force of gravity on the plane is still pulling straight down. This means that in a turn, the lift made by the wings isn't as effective at countering the force of gravity.

What if a pilot is flying in the mountains and sees a high ridge and a peak in front of her? To get around the peak and over the ridge, she has to turn and climb at the same time. But in a turn, the plane's wings will create less lift. So she has to find a way to make more lift while she turns, so she can climb. Think about what you've read so far. What could this pilot do to get more lift from the wings?

If you said she could raise the angle of the wings (angle of attack), you're right. Raising the angle of attack of a wing creates more lift. What else? The pilot could add more power. That would cause the plane to go faster, which would put more air over the wings. More air and faster speed also create more lift.

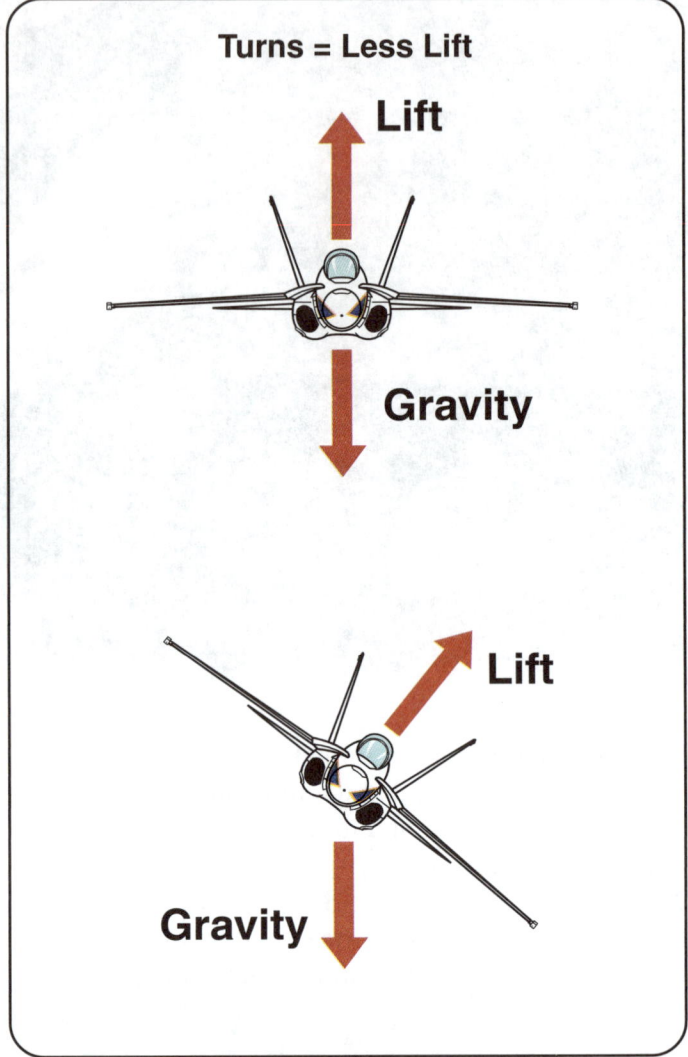

NASA photo

Photo courtesy of Six Flags Magic Mountain

G-Forces

Turning an airplane sharply can also create what's known as "G," or "gravity" forces. Think about what happens if you're in a car that's travelling quickly down an S-turn road. You get thrown side to side as the car goes around the turns. This is because the movement of the car creates a force on your body that is similar to gravity. The same thing happens on a roller coaster. When you swoop through the bottom of a run, you might feel squished into your seat, because the movement of the roller coaster is creating a force that not only acts like gravity, but can be several times as powerful.

The same thing happens in an airplane. The movement of a sharp turn can create a force on the plane and its passengers that is measured in how many times the normal force of gravity it exerts on a person. When people talk about fighter pilots pulling 6 "G's," they mean that the speed and turning of the airplane create a force equal to six times the normal pull of gravity. So a 200 pound pilot will feel as if he weighs 1,200 pounds! The plane will also feel six times as much as the normal force of gravity pulling on it. So if a plane is being designed for high "G" turns, its wings have to be extra sturdy, or they might break.

Young Eagles

Want to see for yourself how the forces of flight feel? You can – through the EAA Aviation Foundation's Young Eagles Program. Since it began in 1992, the Young Eagles Program has introduced more than half a million young people ages 8 –17 to the world of flight. The program matches up people like you who want to fly with qualified, volunteer pilots in your local area who want to share their love of the sky. It's easy, and it's the experience of a lifetime. For more information, contact the EAA Young Eagles office at 877-806-8902, email the program at yeagles@eaa.org, or look at the Young Eagles website: www.youngeagles.org.

Photos courtesy of EAA

General Chuck Yeager, Honorary Chairman, EAA Young Eagles

Stability

Letting the air out of a balloon gives it a lot of thrust, but it has no stability or control. It just careens all over the room. A leaf floating through the air has lift, but it won't necessarily stay right side up, and you can't steer it anywhere. It isn't stable or controllable.

To be useful, an airplane not only has to have lift and thrust, it has to be stable, and it has to be controllable — in three dimensions! Cars only go right and left, but airplanes move in three different directions, or **axes** (áx-ees) as aeronautical engineers would say.

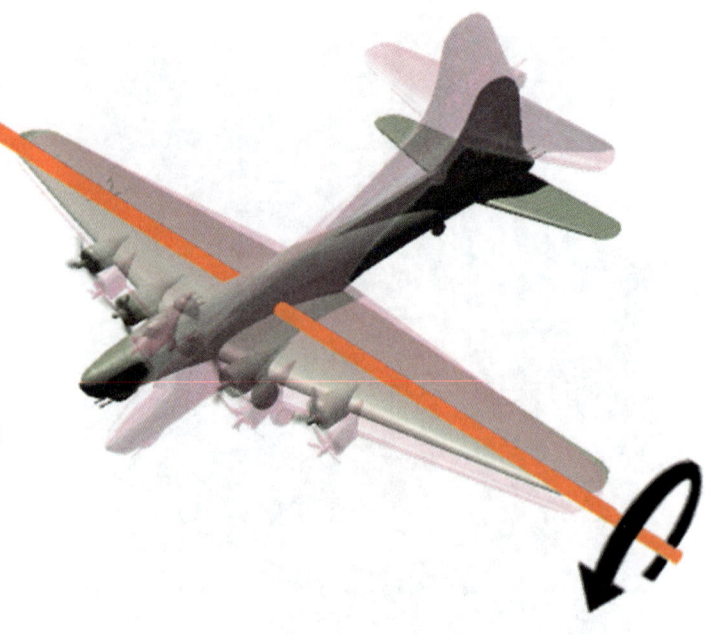

An airplane can **pitch** up or down, meaning it can raise or lower its nose. If a pilot keeps raising the airplane's nose, the plane will loop all the way around.

A plane can **roll** by raising its left or right wing. If a pilot keeps raising one wing far enough, the plane will roll upside down and all the way around until it's top-side up again.

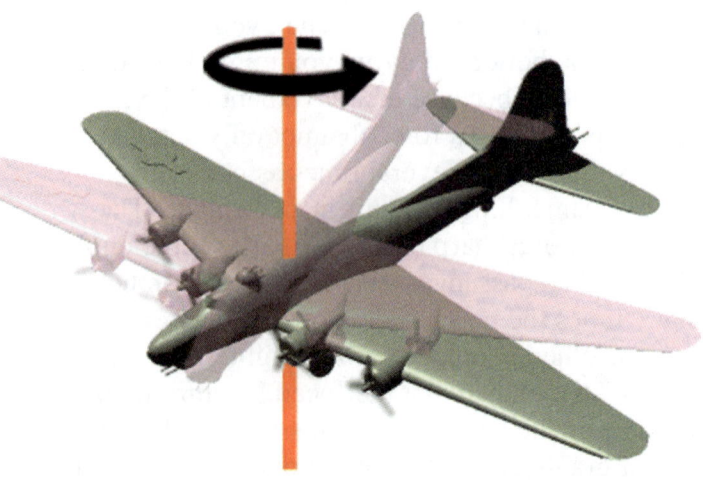

A plane can **yaw** left of right by moving the tail of the plane left or right. The plane stays level if it's yawing. It just changes the direction it's heading because the tail is swinging around.

Making an Airplane Stable

The first thing designers do is add wings, which help keep the plane right side up. Any wing would help make a plane more stable, but if you look at most airplanes head-on, you'll also notice that their wings angle up slightly toward the tips, in a slight "V" shape with the fuselage. This angle is called a **dihedral** (die-hée-dral), and it helps keep the plane right side up. How? If the plane starts to roll to the right, the top of the left wing won't be facing up, but the top of the right wing still will be. So the lift created by the right wing will be more effective than the lift created by the left wing. This will make the plane want to roll back to a level position.

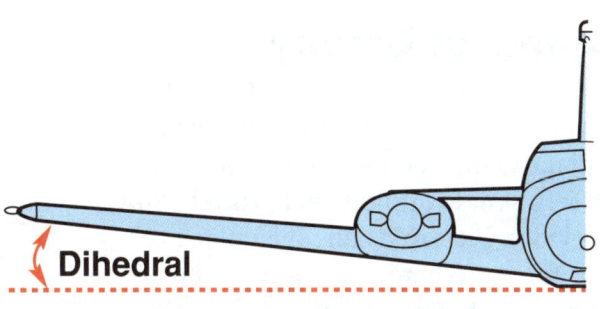

Dihedral makes a wing stable.

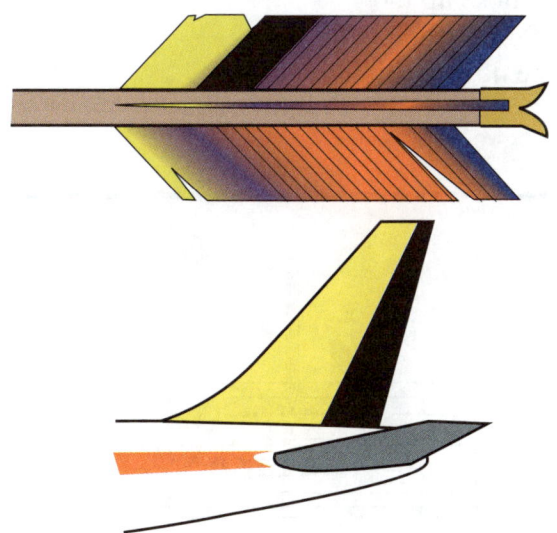

The vertical tail of an airplane acts like the tail feathers of an arrow.

The next thing designers do to make a plane stable is add a vertical tail. This helps keep the airplane pointed straight ahead, just as the feathers on an arrow or the keel of a boat help keep the arrow or boat pointing straight forward. Think about it. An arrow without feathers would spin out of control. Likewise, a boat with a flat bottom would skitter around in all directions. (Test this with a bathtub toy!) But a boat with a keel that sticks down in the water will track ahead in a fairly straight line. Remember that the air flowing over a plane is a fluid, like water. So the vertical tail of an airplane works the same way as the keel of the boat. Aeronautical engineers call this **directional stability**.

The third thing designers do to make a plane stable is add a second horizontal surface — either a horizontal tail or a forward **canard** — to keep the plane from pitching up or down too far. Most wings have a slight upward angle, while horizontal tails, or stabilizers, have a slight downward angle. So the horizontal stabilizer works to balance the lifting force of the wings. With the two surfaces, the airplane is much more stable in pitch. (To find out how a forward canard can achieve this same effect, read the "Variations on Control Surfaces" section.)

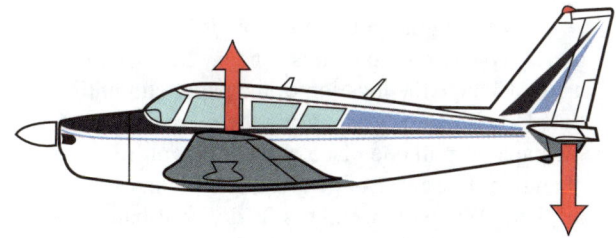

A horizontal tail balances the lift produced by an airplane's wing.

Balance

Center of Gravity

To be stable, a plane also has to be well-balanced. Somewhere in the middle of the airplane is the central pivot point for all its different kinds of movement (**pitch**, **roll** and **yaw**). Picture balancing a plane on your finger. Where your finger is balancing the plane is the **center of gravity**. It's important in airplane design and flying to keep this point close to where most of the lift is being created, or the **center of lift** (usually, this **center of lift** is near the thickest part of the wing).

If the center of gravity, or weight, is *behind* the center of lift, it will make the plane tail-heavy, which might force the plane's nose up too high to fly. If the center of gravity is in *front* of the center of lift, the plane will be nose-heavy, in which case a pilot might not be able to get the nose up high enough to fly.

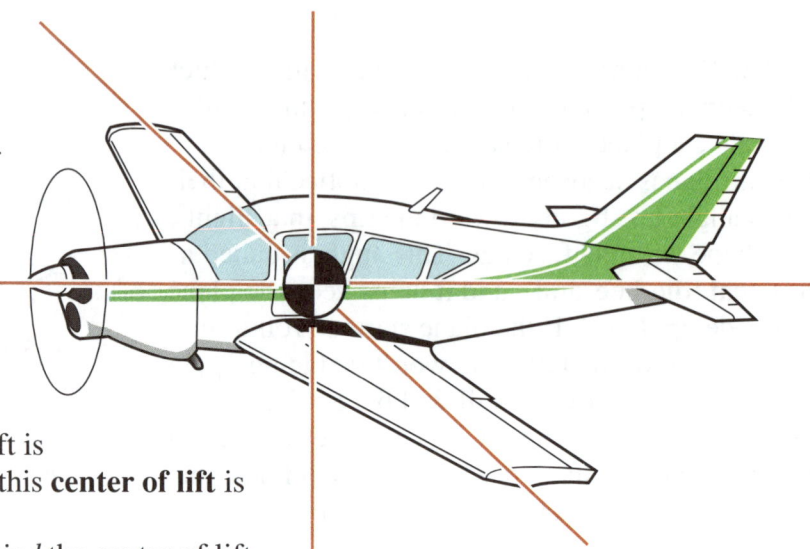

NASA Glider

Want to see for yourself how the center of gravity affects how an airplane flies? Building this Styrofoam glider will show you. (Template for the glider is on page 159)

Trace the glider template onto a Styrofoam tray, and cut out the 3 separate pieces. Use a piece of sandpaper or a nail file to smooth the edges. Cut the two slots in the plane's body (or fuselage) as marked, and slide the wing and horizontal tail into those slots.

Try flying the glider. See how it flies. Now attach a paper clip to its nose and try throwing it again. Change the location of the paper clip until the plane flies well. By adding the extra weight of the paper clip in one place or another, you're changing the **center of gravity**, or weight, of the airplane. When the weight is finally well-balanced, with the center of gravity near the center of the plane, the glider will fly well.

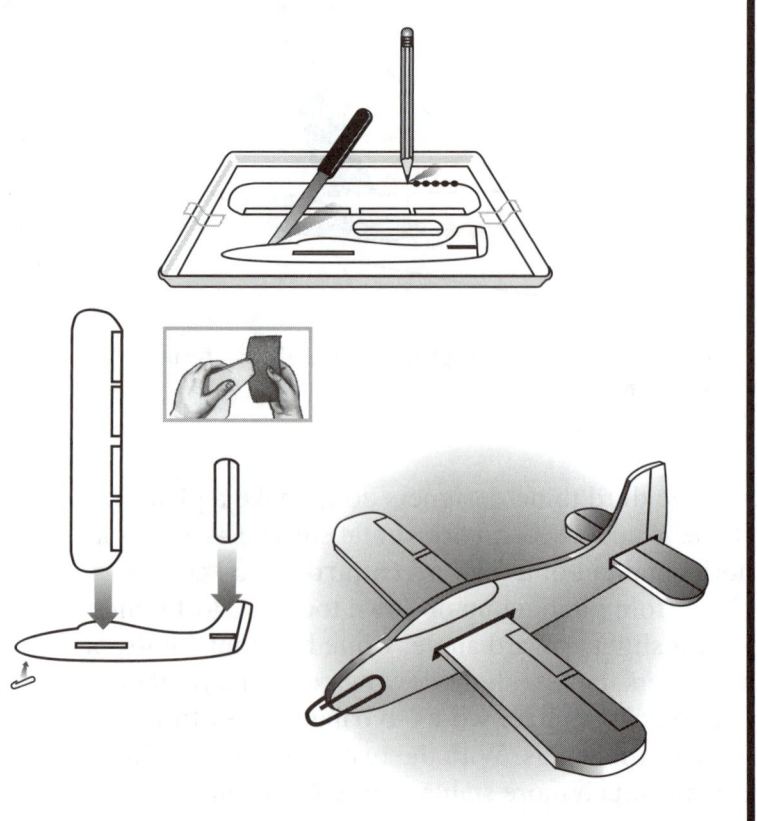

Photo courtesy of Raytheon Aircraft and Paul Bowen

A Case of Balance: The Beech Starship

This unusual-looking turboprop business plane is called the Beech Starship, and it illustrates how center of gravity problems can affect an airplane's design. The Starship has two wing surfaces: a forward wing (or canard), and a main wing. This is because the designers wanted the spar of the wing to go through the airplane behind the passenger cabin, in order to make the cabin roomier for the passengers. The problem with this design is that it would put most of the weight (the passengers) and the center of gravity in *front* of the wing and the center of lift. This would make the plane nose-heavy. So the designers added a small forward wing, called a canard, to create more lift at the front of the plane. This kept the plane's weight and lift balanced. (For more on canards, read the section on "Variations on Control Surfaces.")

© Kurt Hoy

Real Life Profile: Mike Jacoby
World Champion Snowboarder, Pilot, Underwood, WA

When Mike Jacoby was a kid, he didn't think he could be a pilot because he had a hearing problem. But that didn't stop him from trying to get airborne any way he could. He started snowboarding, and he was soon catching air all the way to six world snowboarding titles. He made the 1998 Olympic snowboarding team and placed 17th in the Giant Slalom.

Then he found out his hearing problem wasn't bad enough to keep him from becoming a pilot. He now owns a Piper Comanche, which he uses to get to great snowboarding and surfing locations. "I like the freedom of flying, and I like the freedom it gives me to go places," he says.

Jacoby's also found out something he wished he'd known as a kid: most pilots love to give people rides. "I didn't have a lot of money as a kid, so flying seemed pretty out of reach," he says. "But pilots like to give kids a chance. If kids come and hang out or work at the airport, they can learn to fly that way."

Control

Making an airplane stable is important. But for a plane to be useful, it also has to be controllable. Pilots have to be able to command it to climb, descend, turn, or head in a particular direction.

In the earliest days of flight, the Wright brothers designed a crude system of twisting, or "warping" the plane's wings to control their plane. **Wing warping** works kind of like an acrobatic kite. To "steer" an acrobatic kite, you pull a string on one side or the other. The string twists one side of the kite down, which makes the kite turn. The first "Wright Flyer" airplane worked very much like that.

Most modern planes, however, rely on separate, moveable **control surfaces** to make an airplane turn, climb or descend. A conventional airplane has three different types of control surfaces:

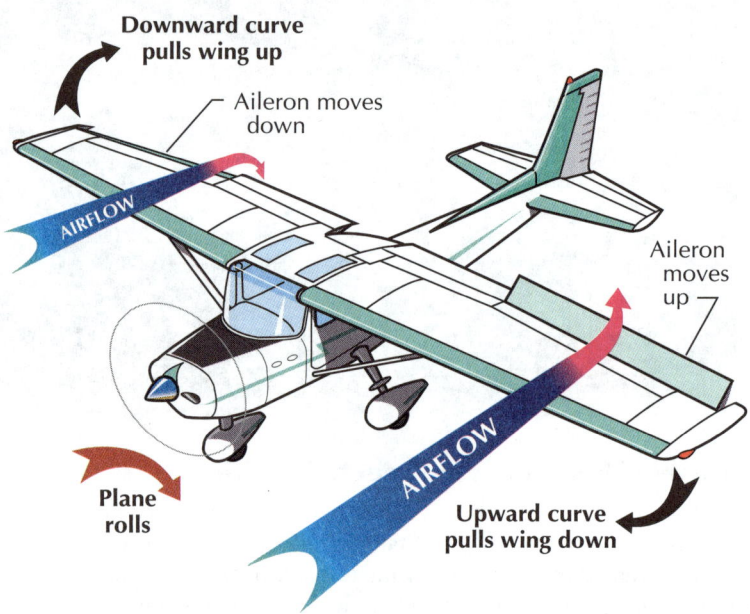

1) **Ailerons**. These moveable surfaces are located along the back edge of the wings. When a pilot turns the control yoke to the right, the aileron on the right wing goes up and the one on the left wing goes down. This makes the airplane **roll** to the right. How? When the right aileron moves up, it creates a curve *under* the right wing. And when the left aileron moves down, it creates a bigger curve on *top* of the left wing. Since a curved surface creates low pressure above it, and objects want to move toward the low pressure, the right wing will want to go down, and the left wing will want to go up. This rolls the airplane to the right.

Weird Control Surfaces

NASA Photo

Flying Wing
This "Flying Wing" was designed in the 1940s. Today's B-2 is a descendant of this plane. It has no tail, so all the control surfaces have to be incorporated into the trailing edge of the wing. To see how this odd airplane flies, read "Variations on Control Surfaces."

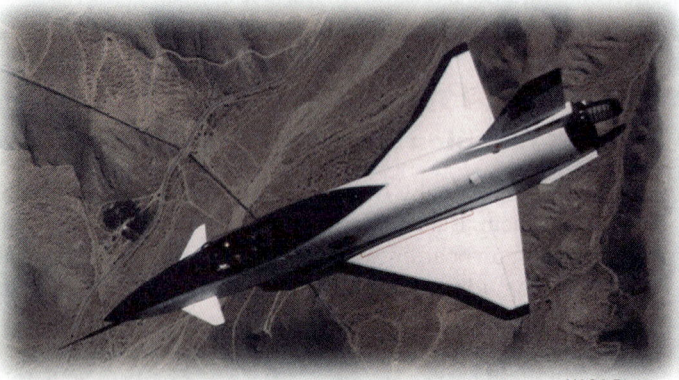

NASA Photo

X-31
This NASA X-31 research aircraft doesn't have a horizontal stabilizer — its ailerons and elevators are both on the trailing edge of its wing. But what's REALLY odd about its control system is that it can change the angle of its engine exhaust to make it turn more quickly. To see how this works, read the section on "Thrust Vectoring."

2) **Rudder**. This is the moveable surface on the back of the vertical tail. A rudder works just like a vertical aileron. When the pilot presses on the left rudder pedal, it moves the rudder to the left. This gives the right side of the rudder a greater curve. This, in turn, creates lower pressure on the right side of the rudder, which makes the tail move to the right. If the tail of the airplane moves right, the nose will move to the left. This is called **yaw**. And it's how the rudder works with the ailerons to help turn the plane.

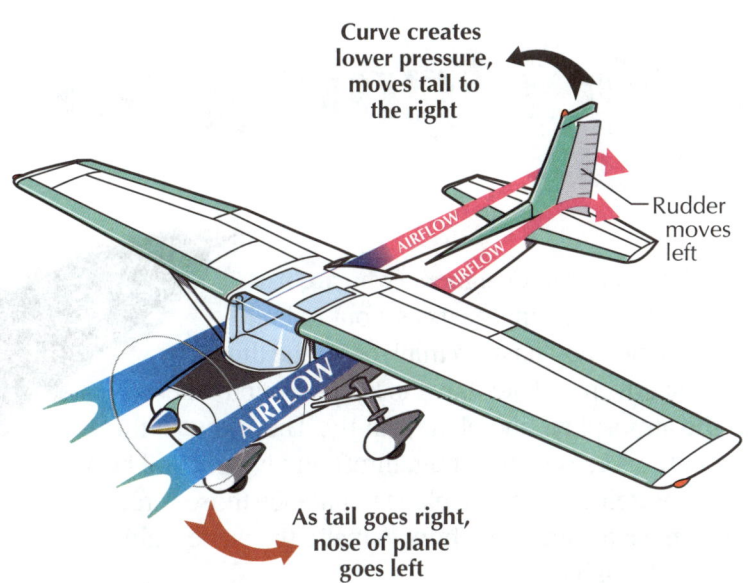

3) **Elevator**. This is the moveable surface on the back edge of the horizontal stabilizer (on the airplane's tail). It controls the airplane's **pitch**. To descend, the pilot pushes forward on the control yoke or stick. That makes the elevator go *down*. This gives the top of the horizontal stabilizer a bigger curve, which creates a lower pressure area above it. Since objects move toward areas of low pressure, this makes the tail of the airplane go *up*, which makes the nose of the airplane go down. To climb, the pilot pulls back on the stick. This makes the elevator go *up*, which makes the tail go *down*. That pulls the nose of the airplane up.

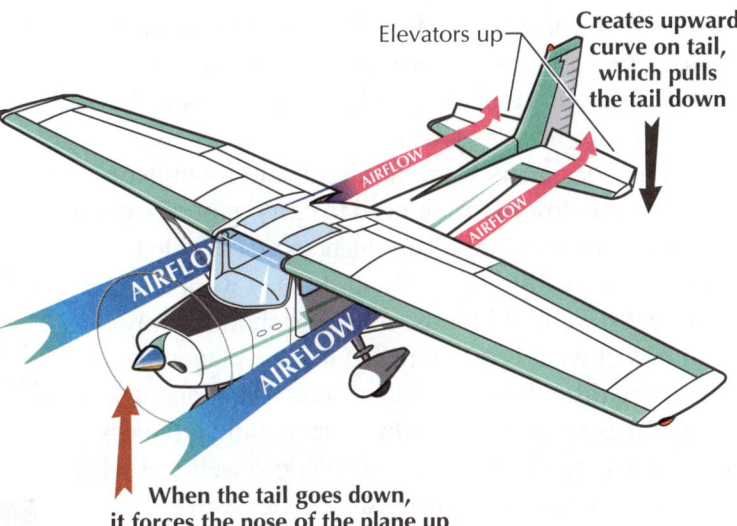

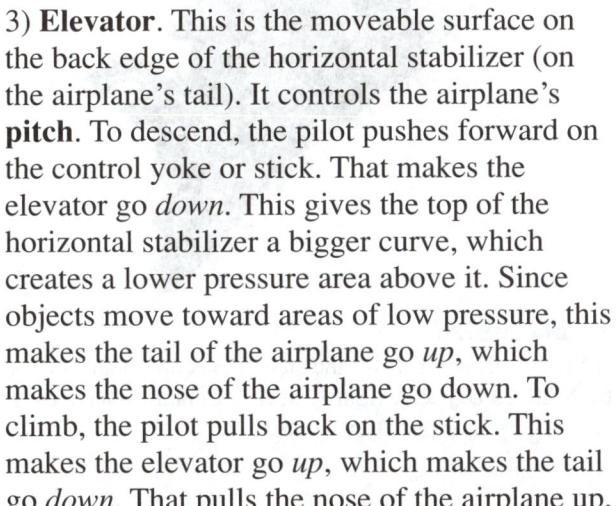

Photo courtesy of EAA

Canard

Some newer airplanes have their wings further back, and a small wing-like surface at the nose of the plane. (See the box on the Beech Starship in the previous section). These forward wings are called *canards*, and they sometimes control pitch, as well. For more information on how canards work, see the "Variations on Control Surfaces" section.

NASA Photo

X-1

Among the many things the X-1 taught engineers was that supersonic planes would go out of control if they had a conventional horizontal stabilizer and elevator. So the X-1 was modified to have a **stabilator**, or "all-flying tail." The whole horizontal tail acts as the elevator and moves up and down to control the airplane's pitch. To find out more about the X-1 read the section on "Supersonic Airplanes."

33

Designing an Airplane

When aircraft designers (who are usually aeronautical engineers) set out to build an airplane, they have to think of all the things we just covered. They have to keep in mind where in the atmosphere the plane will fly. They have to think about the forces of lift, drag, thrust and weight and how they are going to get the plane to balance those forces. They have to figure out how to make the plane stable and controllable.

But the first thing they have to figure out is what they want the airplane to do. Why? Because no airplane can do everything well. Airplanes are designed to do specific jobs, and a plane's design will be very different depending on what its job is.

Do the designers want the airplane to fly high or low? Fast or slow? Does it need to carry a lot of weight or does it just need to be very maneuverable? Do they want it to be really easy to fly, or do they want it to perform really well? Will it use a long or short runway?

Look at what is different about these planes and why those differences might be there. Think about what each of these planes has to do. What could you guess about what the SR-71's wing shape does well and what the Cessna 172 training wing shape does well?

Read on, and you'll find out what all sorts of wings do, and get ideas for your own wild airplane designs!

SR-71 "Blackbird"
Does an SR-71 "Blackbird" — the sleek black spy plane still flown by NASA's Dryden Flight Research Center — have to carry a lot of cargo, or just fly very fast?

C-130 "Hercules"
Does a "Dumbo Drop" C-130 cargo plane have to go very fast, or just carry a lot?

Cessna 172
What is important for an airplane that will be used to teach students how to fly? Does it have to go fast? Or is it more important that it's gentle and easy to fly?

F-18 Hornet
What does a fighter like this NASA F-18 need to do well?

MD-11 Airliner
What does this MD-11 need to do well?

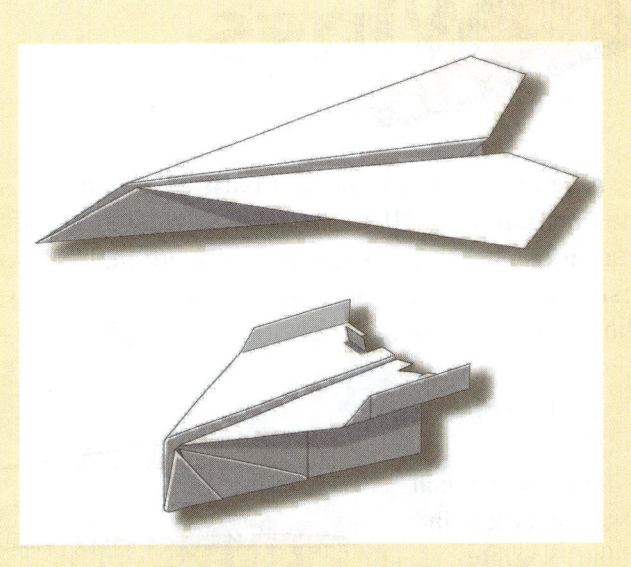

Speed vs. Maneuverability

Even paper airplane designers know they have to give planes different wings to do different jobs. Look at these two paper airplane designs. One is designed to go fast, and the other is designed to be "maneuverable," so it can do loops and rolls. See how different they look? It's the same with real airplanes.

Neat Fact: If the curve of an airplane wing is what creates **lift**, how does a flat paper airplane wing fly? The answer is **angle of attack**. When you throw the paper airplane, you give it a slightly positive angle of attack — its nose is above its flight path. Remember how this makes the wing "act" as if it has a bigger curve, even with a real airplane? With a paper airplane, this is what gives the wing its basic curve, and what makes it able to create lift and fly!

Real Life Profile: Trier Brown
19 Years Old, Lockheed Lightspeed Graduate/Volunteer
Palmdale, CA

The famous Lockheed "Skunk Works" in Palmdale, CA has designed lots of amazing planes over the years. Some of the best engineers in the country work there. But several times a year, middle school students also get to spend a weekend at the Skunk Works. Through Lockheed's "Lightspeed" program, students can learn about airplane design, rocket engines, and even how to build a "deceleration" system to keep an egg from breaking if it's dropped off a balcony. Students apply for the program simply by writing an essay saying why they want to attend.

Trier Brown went through the program when she was in 8th grade and liked it so much that she asked to come back as a volunteer. Her experiences also got her excited enough about designing and flying airplanes that she's going to the Naval Academy to become a Navy pilot.

"I think a lot of kids look at aviation and think it looks so far fetched for them to actually do," she says. "But it's not."

Wings

One of the most important parts of an airplane — and one that has a HUGE impact on what kinds of work it can do — is its wings. There are many things designers can change on a wing so it will do things like create more **lift**, fly better at high **angles of attack**, fly faster, stand the heat of re-entering the Earth's atmosphere, or stay in the air a long time at high altitude. Some of the main things engineers look at in designing a plane's wings are:

1. Wing camber
Wing camber refers to how much curve there is in the wing. Remember that a bigger curve creates more lift — but a thicker, rounder wing also creates more drag. A thinner, flatter wing will cut through the air better.

2. Aspect ratio
Aspect ratio is the *length* of the wing compared to its *width*. A long, narrow wing is called a **high aspect ratio** wing, and it will generally create more lift with less drag. But if you want a plane to go very fast and turn quickly, you want a shorter, wider wing (like fighter planes have) — or one with a **low aspect ratio**.

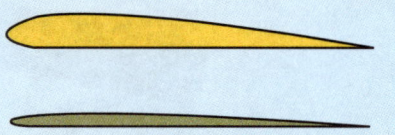

Low aspect ratio wing

High aspect ratio wing

3. Wing planform
The wing planform refers to the shape of the wings if you were looking down on them from above. The wings might be swept back at an angle, or they might be shaped like a triangle. They could be straight and rectangular or have an elliptical (a long oval) kind of shape. They might be straight and tapered (narrower at the outer tip than at the root, near the airplane's fuselage), or they might even be swept forward. Each different shape has its advantages and disadvantages. Which one a designer picks depends on what the airplane has to do well.

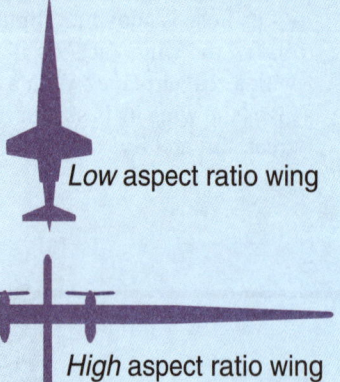

4. Wing area
Wing area is the total surface area of the wing. Generally, the bigger a wing is, the more lift it will create. But a big wing may also create more drag and weigh more.

5. Wing loading
Wing loading is a direct result of wing area. It means how much weight each square foot of wing has to lift. A small wing is faster, because it causes less drag. But if a plane has a smaller wing, then every square foot of that wing has to lift more weight in order to make the airplane fly. This means that if there are two planes that weigh the same, the plane with the smaller wing will have a *higher wing loading*. High wing loading generally means the plane will need higher speeds to takeoff, fly and land, because it will need a lot of air going over its wing to create enough lift to carry the higher load.

6. Smoothness
Air will flow more easily over a smoother wing. It will also "stick" to a smooth wing better instead of burbling off of bumps, rivets, and sharp edges. Since lift is only created when air is flowing smoothly over a wing, a smooth wing will create more lift and less drag. This means that the airplane can go faster, or will use less fuel to go the same speed, than a plane with a bumpier wing. The smoothest kind of wing is called a **laminar flow** wing. Making a wing this smooth is difficult, however, so if a plane doesn't have to go fast, designers may not worry about keeping a wing smooth.

Swept Wing vs Straight Wing

This Cessna 150, which is used to teach students how to fly, was designed with a much more stable, rectangular wing shape.

This Cessna Citation X business jet has a "swept" wing that angles backwards. A swept wing allows a plane to go faster. But it doesn't perform as well at low speeds and can be more difficult to handle in the air.

Wing Loading

This NASA F-104 fighter plane weighs 29,000 pounds and has a wing area of 196 square feet. This means its wing loading is about **147** pounds per square foot (each square foot of wing has to lift 147 pounds).

This Piper Super Cub has about the same wing areaas a F-104, but it only weighs 1,850 pounds. So the Cub has a wing loading of less than **9** pounds per square foot. This means the Cub wing doesn't have to create as much lift per square foot to make the airplane fly. So the Cub can keep flying even at very slow speeds. The Cub can land at **40** miles an hour, while the F-104 lands at over **140** miles an hour. So while the F-104 needs a very long runway, the Cub can land on a short gravel bar in a river!

Training Wings

The most simple and basic kind of wing is the kind used on airplanes that are used for flight instruction ("trainers"). This kind of wing has a large **camber**, or curve, which means the wing will produce good lift even at slow speeds. Why? Because a big curve in the airfoil means that the air has to divert more to go up and around the upper surface of the wing, which speeds up the air and creates a very low pressure area above the wing. This means the wing will create more lift even when the plane is flying level or doesn't have much air going over the wing.

A wing that can fly at slow speeds is important in a training airplane, because instructors want students to have time to process and figure out what needs to be done next. An airplane that flies slower lets a student have that kind of time.

It's also important for a training wing to be docile — kind of like the old nag horse in the stable that you'd put someone on the first time they went riding. A fast thoroughbred horse might win the Kentucky Derby, but you wouldn't want to have to *learn* how to ride on a jumpy, difficult-to-handle thoroughbred. It's the same thing with planes.

What makes a wing "docile"? A couple of things. First, a straight wing is more docile than a swept-back wing, so training wings are usually straight.

When a straight wing stalls, the air usually stops flowing over the wing at the **root**, near the airplane's fuselage, first. This means that although the wing will stop making lift there and the nose of the airplane will drop, air will still be flowing over the outside portions of the wing, which is where the **ailerons** are. So the whole wing doesn't stall at once, and the pilot can still control the wing, even as it starts to stall. This makes a plane with a straight wing much easier and safer to fly.

To make sure that the wing root stalls before the tip, designers also often put a slight twist in the wing, so the outside tip of the wing is angled slightly more downward, or forward, than the root of the wing. So the **angle of attack** (the angle above the plane's flight path) of the wing tip will always be lower than that of the wing root. This insures that air will stop flowing over the wing root before it stops at the wing tips.

Cessna 172

Look-down view of a Cessna 172 wing.

Cross-section of a Cessna 172 wing, showing airfoil.

Photo courtesy of EAA

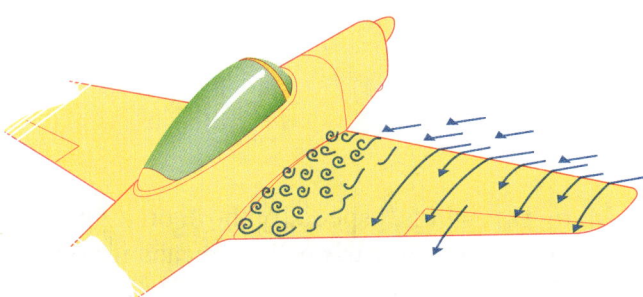

This illustration shows a wing beginning to stall at the "root," near the fuselage. The tufts of yarn no longer lie flat, because air is no longer flowing smoothly over that part of the wing.

This Stearman biplane was a training airplane in the 1930s and 1940s. Its wing is thick and has a pronounced camber, or curve, which means it will fly and land well at slow speeds. Trainers don't need to be efficient or fast, just easy to fly.

Training wings can be attached to an airplane in different ways. This Cessna 172 has a high wing, while this Grumman Tiger has a low wing. There are some differences between the two, but both wings behave in a similar manner.

Tapered Wing Cessna 172

Straight Wing Grumman Tiger

A Tapered Training Wing

Some trainers, like a newer Cessna 172, have a straight wing that tapers slightly at the tips. This is a compromise to make the wing a little faster and more efficient, by tapering the wings at the tips, while keeping its stall characteristics docile by keeping a straight, square shape at the wing root. The straight, square shape at the root will make the wing stall there first, which is what you want on a training airplane.

Fast Wings

What if you want to design a plane that goes REALLY FAST? You don't want to put a training wing on it. You want performance. Speed. Zip.

To make a wing go fast, you need as little drag as possible. How do you do this? Look at the wings of some jets at your local airport, and you'll begin to get an idea.

Fast wings need to be small, thin, and smooth, so they slip easily through the air molecules. A small, thin wing won't create as much lift as a thick, round one, but you're designing this airplane to go fast, so you're counting on having a lot of air flowing over the wing to make enough lift for the airplane to fly. The plane will have to be moving faster in order to take off, and the wing will **stall**, or lose its **lift**, at a much higher speed. And if it takes off and lands at higher speeds, the plane will need to use much longer runways to speed up and slow down.

Many fast wings, especially those on high-speed jets, also have a **swept wing**. This means if you looked down on the wing from above, the front or leading edge of it would be swept back at an angle. What does a swept wing do? For one thing, a swept wing offers less resistance as it pushes through the air at high speeds than a straight wing does.

A swept wing also slows down the air going over it, which actually helps a wing fly faster, strange as that may seem. How? If a plane is flying *near* the speed of sound, the sped-up air flowing over its wing may actually go *faster* than the speed of sound. (This happens because air going over the top of a wing speeds up, remember?) If the air going over the wing goes faster than the speed of sound, it creates a shock wave, disturbing the air flowing over the wing and causing drag. If the air flowing over the wing can be slowed down a little so that a shock wave

Photo courtesy of Cessna Aircraft Company

Cessna Citation X

Look-down view of a Citation X wing.

Cross-section of a Citation X wing, showing airfoil.

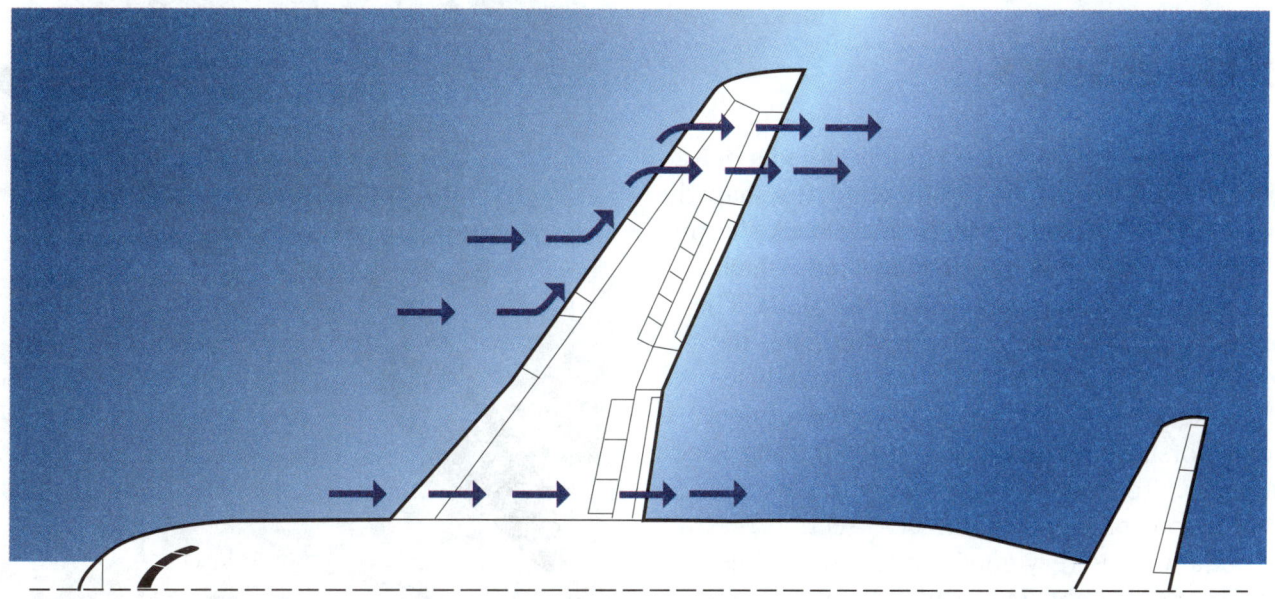

Airflow over a swept wing

doesn't form, it reduces the drag and lets the plane go faster. (To find out more about shock waves, read the section on "Supersonic Flight.")

How does a swept wing slow down the air? The wider (front to back) a wing is, the more the air will speed up as it flows across it. But air flowing over a swept wing doesn't go straight back across the wing. It first moves toward the wing tip along the front edge of the wing and *then* part of it flows back across the wing. Since a swept wing gets narrower toward the wing tip, the air is flowing back across the wing at a narrower spot. This means the air will not speed up as much. So the air won't go supersonic or form a shock wave until the plane is going at a higher speed.

Fast wings are also generally short, especially if the plane has to be maneuverable at high speeds. If you want to go really fast — and especially if you want to go supersonic — you want a wing that's shorter and wider (a **low aspect ratio** wing).

NASA photos

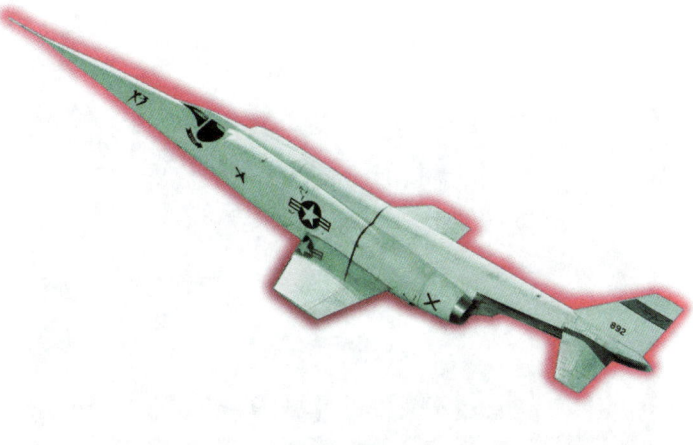

This is the X-15. It was a rocket plane that flew in the 1960s, and it went faster than any plane ever built — almost 7 times the speed of sound. That's over 4,000 miles an hour! Neil Armstrong, the first person to walk on the moon, flew one of these at NASA's Dryden Flight Research Center before he became an astronaut. Look how tiny its wing is. It had to be that small in order for the plane to go that fast.

The X-3 was an experimental research plane flown at NASA's Dryden Flight Research Center in the 1950s. It had a long, thin fuselage and a very thin, tiny wing, which let it cut through the air easily and fast. The wing also had a low aspect ratio (was shorter in length and wider from front to back), which made it good for very high speed flight.

Delta Wings

An extreme kind of swept wing is called a **delta wing**. If you look down on a delta wing, it's shaped like a triangle. The leading edges angle back sharply until they meet the back edge of the wing, which goes straight across the back end of the plane. The advantage of a delta wing is that it eliminates the need for a separate horizontal tail, which reduces drag (one less thing sticking out from the airplane). The elevators are incorporated into the trailing edge of the wing. (To find out exactly how this works, see the "Variations on Control Surfaces" section.)

A delta wing is very good for very high-speed dashes or cruise flight. This is why the Supersonic Transport "Concorde" and the SR-71 "Blackbird" have delta wings. Both planes were designed to do one thing — fly fast.

But one disadvantage of a delta wing is that it doesn't maneuver as well as a conventional swept wing design. So while the Concorde has a delta wing, most U.S. military jet fighters are designed with a more conventional swept wing and a separate horizontal tail. Delta wings also land a lot faster than other swept wings designs. (For more information on why this is true, read the section on "Supersonic Flight.")

The SR-71 "Blackbird"

The Convair F-102A "Delta Dagger" was the first American delta-wing fighter.

NASA photos

The Mach 2 "Tu-144" supersonic transport.

The F-16XL — a research plane flown by the Air Force and NASA.

Nemesis Formula 1 Racer

Photo courtesy of EAA

Fast Wings Aren't Always Jets! The Nemesis Racer

This composite Formula 1 racer, called "Nemesis," was built by a couple of friends in a hangar at their local airport. It raced at 260 mph, which was so fast for its size that it wasn't beaten in a race from 1991 until it was retired in July 2000. It held the national championship title in its class for almost 10 years and set numerous speed records. What was the plane's secret? One secret was its fast wings. It had very smooth, **laminar flow** wings, which had very little drag. It also had a unique wing shape. The wing had a cusp, or upward curve, along its back edge. This created a high-pressure area at the back edge of the wing which helped push the airplane faster through the air. Think of how a slippery pumpkin seed shoots forward when you squeeze it in between two fingers, and you'll get the idea of how this high pressure cusp works.

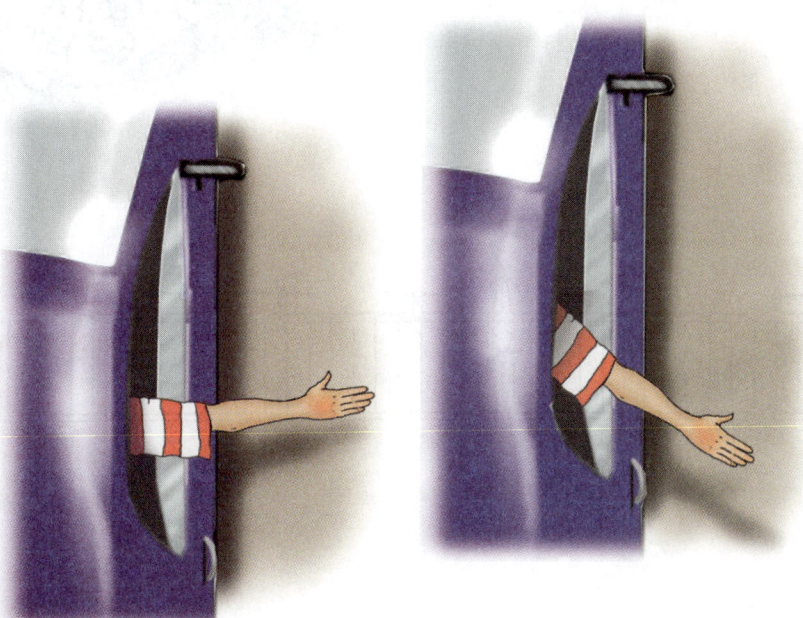

Swept Wing Dynamics

Want to see for yourself how a swept wing helps a plane cut through the air better at high speeds? Try sticking your arm straight out the window of your family car when it's going slow. Now let your arm trail backward some (so your arm is like a swept wing). Feel the difference in the air flow and force over your arm.

Now try this again (carefully) while the car is moving faster. You'll notice that there's a lot more force pushing on your arm when it's out straight than when it's swept back. This illustrates one of the advantages of swept-back wings. At high speeds, a swept wing offers less resistance to cutting through the air.

Long Range Wings

What if you need an airplane to stay up in the air a long time? Say you wanted to build a glider. A glider has to be very good at making lift in order to fly, because it doesn't have an engine to give it any thrust or keep air flowing over its wings. Or maybe you need a plane to fly for long periods of time high up in the atmosphere where the air is very thin, so you can take spy photos or collect data from the air up there. Or maybe you need a plane to cross the Pacific Ocean — or go around the world — without landing to get any more fuel.

In order to build a plane that could do any of these things, you'd need wings that were very efficient — ones that create a lot of lift without a lot of drag. A very thick wing with a rounded leading edge will create a lot of lift, but it's got a big frontal area that has to plow through the air, which means it also has a lot of drag. A very long, narrow wing, on the other hand, can create lift all the way down the wing, so the curve of its wing doesn't have to be as big to create a lot of lift.

A lot of different types of planes use long-range wings to accomplish a lot of missions. The planes are made of very different materials, but they all **high aspect ratio** wings — which means they are all very long and narrow.

NASA photo

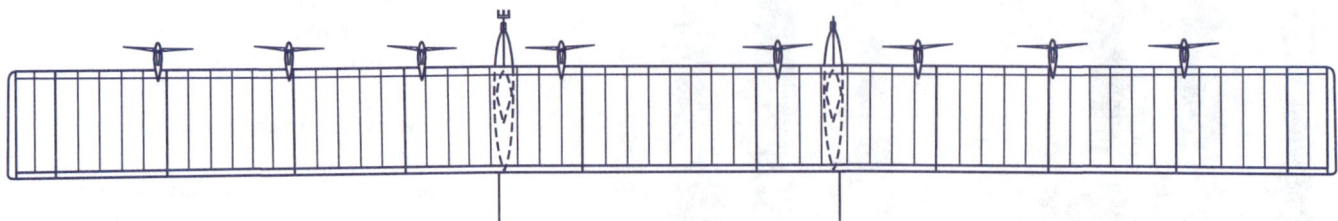

Look-down view of the Pathfinder wing shape.

The Pathfinder

The designers of this Pathfinder research aircraft had a very specific goal. They wanted to build an airplane that could fly at very high altitudes for a VERY long time. To do this, they decided to put solar powered motors on the plane, so it wouldn't have to land to refuel. (For more on these engines, read the section on "Alternative Fuel Engines.")

But even the best solar engines could only make and store enough power to keep the Pathfinder aloft if the plane was very light and created a lot of lift. So the Pathfinder's wing is long and narrow. Its 100 foot length is longer than the wing of a Boeing 737 airliner, but the Pathfinder's wing is only 8 feet wide (from front to back). It was also made of very lightweight materials, so even though it has a wing area of 800 square feet (100 ft x 8 ft), it only weighs 400 pounds. This gives the Pathfinder a wing loading of only 1/2 a pound per square foot — lighter than even a Super Cub! The wing is covered in mylar plastic — like the silver mylar balloons you might buy in a store. So it's not terribly rugged or sturdy, and it only flies 15 miles an hour, but it can fly at 65,000 feet for a long time. One thing that makes this super light wing stable enough to fly is the fact that it flexes enough to give it a lot of dihedral (upward angle) when it flies.

What jobs could a plane like the Pathfinder do? Because it's flown remotely (no pilot on board), it could take spy "reconnaissance" photos over enemy territory without having to risk a pilot's life. It could take continuous photos of storms, and collect air samples from the upper atmosphere. It could also take air samples in places where planes with an air-breathing engine can't safely go, like in ash clouds from erupting volcanoes or places where scientists suspect there is nuclear radiation.

Cross-section of Pathfinder wing, showing airfoil shape.

NASA photo

NASA ER-2

This NASA research plane, called the ER-2 (for "Environmental Research-2"), is a modified version of a Lockheed spy plane designed in the 1950s. The original plane was called a "U-2," and one of these airplanes became famous in 1960 when it was shot down over Russia. The plane had a very long, narrow wing because it was designed to fly at high altitudes, where there aren't very many air molecules. Without many air molecules flowing over the wing, the plane had to have a wing shape that would create lift with very little drag. So the wing had to be long, thin, and have a light wing loading (so each square foot of wing would have to create less lift in order for the airplane to fly).

As opposed to the slow Pathfinder, the ER-2 is a jet that can fly over 500 mph. But because it was designed as a very lightweight jet, its wing loading is still relatively low. Its long wings also allow its pilot to shut down its engine and glide for periods of time to save fuel. This ability lets the plane stay aloft longer.

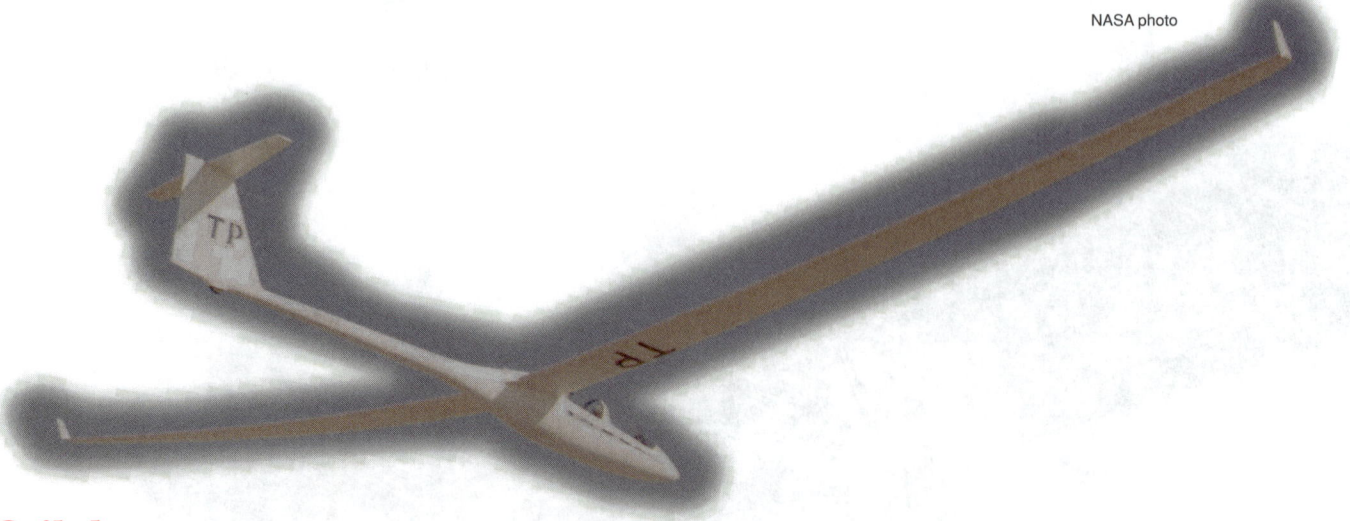

NASA photo

Sailplane

A sailplane is the classic example of a long-endurance or high-altitude wing. It has a very high aspect ratio (long and narrow) wing so it can make the most of the lift it creates. Even though gliders, or sailplanes, have no engines, they sometimes can stay aloft for long periods of time.

Sailplane race pilots sometimes fly 400 miles or more before landing. (For a refresher on how a sailplane can do this, re-read the box on gliders in the "thrust" section.

Photo courtesy of EAA

The Voyager

This unusual-looking airplane was built with one goal in mind: to fly all the way around the world without stopping for fuel. In designing the *Voyager*, speed didn't really matter. Comfort for its pilots didn't really matter. All that really mattered was making the airplane efficient enough to get around the world on one tank of fuel. So its designer gave it extremely long and narrow wings, as well as a very narrow fuselage, to create lift with as little drag as possible. In December 1986, pilots Jeanna Yeager and Dick Rutan flew the airplane all the way around the world — with no stops. It took them nine days. They were the first pilots, and the *Voyager* was the first airplane, to ever accomplish that feat.

Real Life Profile: Mark Hardy
16 years old, Glider Pilot, Chicago, IL

Mark Hardy always dreamed of being a pilot, but he never thought the dream would come true. Hardy's family didn't have the money for him to learn to fly. But a local group called the Aviation Scholarship Foundation gave Hardy a scholarship that allowed him to get his glider pilot's license. And he did so well that the group gave him another scholarship for a powered-plane license.

"Learning to fly's taught me that I really can do anything if I set my mind to it," Hardy says. Flying has also given Hardy a reason to work harder in school, because he now wants to become an Air Force pilot – a goal that requires good grades.

Yet no matter where he ends up, Hardy already has something valuable. "The friendliest community in the world is that of pilots," he says. "And I'm now a pilot. That means I can go to an airport anywhere and be accepted."

Short Take-Off & Landing Wings (STOL)

What if you were flying medical supplies into little villages in the jungles of Central America, a bush pilot taking passengers into remote air strips in the middle of the Alaskan wilderness, or a CIA pilot flying secret supply missions into the mountains of Asia? What would your biggest problem be? Chances are, it would be the size and condition of the landing strips you'd have to use. Hacked out of a jungle or mountainside, your runways would probably be very short, with lots of trees or obstacles around them.

How would you design a plane that could land and take off in a really short distance? Think about it. To take off quickly, a plane would have to have enough lift to fly at a very low speed, so it could take off almost as soon as it started rolling down the runway. And to land in a short distance, the plane would have to be going really slowly when it touched down, so it wouldn't take a lot of distance to stop.

For a plane to fly at really slow speeds, a designer has to figure out a way to keep air flowing smoothly over its wing, even if it's at a high **angle of attack**. The designer also has to figure out how to keep enough air flowing over the control surfaces even at its slowest speeds, so the pilot can still control the plane.

Look-down view of a Super Cub wing shape.

Cross-section of a Super Cub wing, showing airfoil shape.

Piper Super Cub

Photo courtesy of Carey Gray

Planes that can do this are called Short Take off and Landing (STOL) planes. A "STOL" plane would probably have a big engine to help it take off quickly. but it would also probably have a thick wing with a lot of **camber** (curve) in it to create a lot of lift even at slow speeds. It would also have a fairly big **wing area**, making the wing lightly **loaded**, so it wouldn't have to create as much lift to fly.

What else? The plane would probably have big **flaps**, which extend down from the inner portion of the trailing edge of the wing. If a pilot extends the flaps a little bit, it increases the camber, or curve, of the wing, which increases the amount of lift the wing can make. This helps it take off and land at a slower speed. But when most flaps are extended all the way, they act almost like a speed brake. So while a pilot would never use full flaps on take-off, she could use full flaps on landing to slow the airplane down or descend quickly without gaining speed (very useful if she had to come in over treetops and then drop down onto a jungle runway!)

A Piper Super Cub is a good short field airplane. Of course, keep in mind that this kind of plane won't fly very fast, or very high. No plane can do everything.

But is a Super Cub design as good as it gets? No. Aside from the basic wing shape and design, there are numerous things designers can add to make a plane's wing fly even better at slow speeds. These "STOL" modifications make for some amazingly impressive short field approaches!

STOL Modifications

Droop wing tips: Some designers add droop tips to the wings of airplanes to create a curved surface at the end of the wing. This helps air keep flowing smoothly over the tip, making more lift at high angles of attack and slow speeds.

Slots: To keep air from burbling or stalling over the wing at high angles of attack, some designers put a cut, or *slot*, in the wing behind the leading edge, creating a second leading edge of sorts in that area. They also make the angle of the slot's "leading edge" lower than the wing's, so air will continue to flow through the slot and over the wing even when it can't get over the front of the wing anymore.

Slats: Slats are like flaps, except they extend down from the forward, or *leading*, edge of the wing. Like flaps, they make the wing's curve bigger, which lets it create more lift and fly slower.

Droop ailerons: Some STOL airplanes have "droop" ailerons that act almost like flaps. When the flaps are lowered, the ailerons slide back and down a little, as well, making the wing more curved all along the trailing edge.

Wing Fences: Some STOL airplanes have vertical tabs, or "fences" to help funnel slow or potentially burbling air flow straight back over the wing, so the wing and the control surfaces will continue to work even when there isn't much air flowing over them.

Drooped leading edges: Some STOL airplanes are designed with "droopy" leading edges, so when the plane is at a high angle of attack (as it often will be when it's flying extremely slowly), it will be easier for air to keep flowing over it.

Photo courtesy of EAA

Zenair CH-701

Pilatus Porter

Reverse thrust: Some STOL airplanes have jet engines. How can a jet land in a short strip? One way is to use "reverse thrust." This PC-6 Pilatus Porter, for example, is a turboprop, which means it has a propeller, but the propeller is powered by a jet engine, not a piston engine. (To learn more about these engines, read the section on "Jet Engines.") The Porter can land in extremely short distances by changing the angle of its propeller blades, to make them flat (so the prop acts like a big speed brake) or so they push air *forward* instead of back. This pushes the airplane back, helping it to slow down quickly and stop. Many jets also have ways to deflect their thrust forward, helping to stop a plane more quickly.

Real Life Profile: Bob "Hurricane" Hannah
**Motocross Champion, Unlimited Air Racer and Super Cub Pilot
Boise, ID**

Bob "Hurricane" Hannah loves speed. He's won seven national motocross and supercross motorcycle championships. He also raced a P-51 Mustang at almost 500 miles an hour, 50 feet off the deck, at the Reno National Air Races. But his favorite airplane is his little two-seat Super Cub.

The Cub may only go 100 miles an hour, but it lets Hannah have all sorts of adventures in the back country near his Idaho home. Because the Cub has big, high-lift wings, a powerful engine, big flaps and tundra tires, Hannah can land in meadows, on gravel bars, or on top of ridges. He once even landed on a dirt road outside a small town and taxied up to the town's hotel, where he spent the night.

Hannah's Super Cub lets him cruise low and slow, with the window and door open, just about anywhere he wants to go. It may not be as thrilling as his racing, but he says it's every bit as much fun.

Airliner Wings

If you've ever traveled in a commercial airliner and sat by the window, you might have noticed that before take off and landing, parts of the wing extend both forward and backward. Ever wonder why that is? It's the designers' solution to a unique problem that airliners have.

Think about what airliners have to do. They have to carry a lot of weight (passengers, baggage, and fuel). But in order to make airline travel worthwhile, they also have to fly fast once they're off the ground. That's a problem, because high-lift wings generally don't fly very fast.

A plane might be able to have a fast wing and still create enough lift to get a heavy load off the ground if it had huge engines or an unlimited amount of runway on which to build up speed. Likewise, it could keep up enough speed to support that load as it came in for landing if it had 3 or 4 miles in which to slow down and stop once it landed, or if it could use a drag chute like the SR-71 does. But airliners have to operate near cities, on runways that are only 1 1/2 or 2 miles long. While this is long, it's not long enough. And relying on a drag chute to stop every airliner wouldn't be comfortable, practical, or even all that safe.

So designers came up with a way of making airliner wings two different wings in one. When an airliner is in flight, with all the devices on its wing retracted, it's a simple swept wing — a fast wing design.

But for take off and and landing, airliners extend **slats** from the front of the wing and **flaps** from the back side of the wing. These surfaces not only give the wing a much greater curve, they also increase the **area** of the wing. Both of these things help the wing create more lift.

Boeing 737

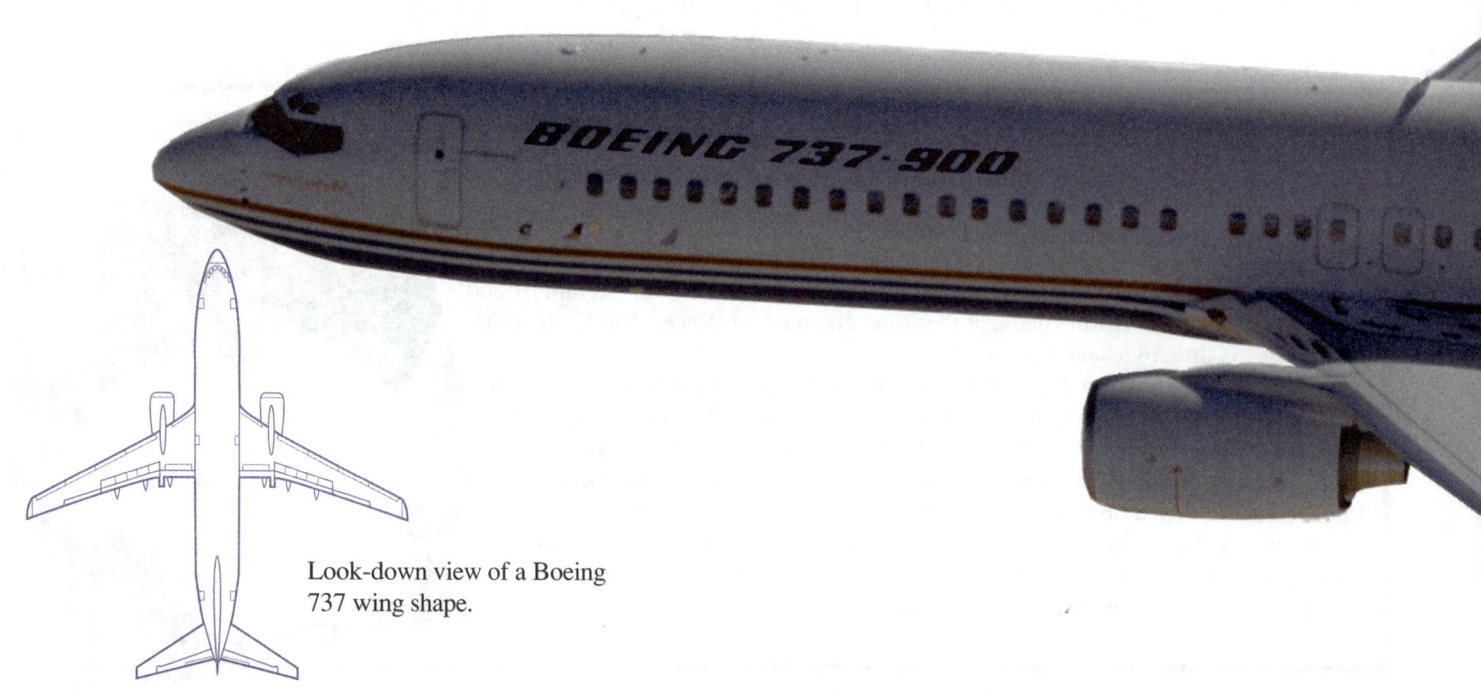

Look-down view of a Boeing 737 wing shape.

NASA photo

Airliners use slats and flaps (below) to maker their wings bigger for take off and landing. They retract those devices (left) to give the plane a faster wing in flight

Photo courtesy of The Boeing Company

Cross-section of a Boeing 737 wing, showing airfoil shape.

Photo courtesy of The Boeing Company

Fowler Flaps

There are different kinds of flaps that airplanes use. With **standard flaps**, a portion of the wing drops down in back. **Split flaps** are attached to the underside of the wing, so the top side of the wing doesn't change when the flap is extended. **Slotted flaps** have a little space between their forward edge and the rest of the wing, so when the flap is extended, it creates a slot similar to a leading edge slot on a STOL airplane. Air can travel from the bottom side of the wing through the slot and over the flap, making it more effective.

Airliners use a different kind of flap, called a **Fowler flap**. When a Fowler flap is extended, it slides *back* as well as *down* on a track and roller system. As it slides back, additional panels of the flap become exposed, increasing the wing's area as well as its curve. This (and a lot of thrust!) is how huge, heavy airliners like a 747 manage to get off the ground.

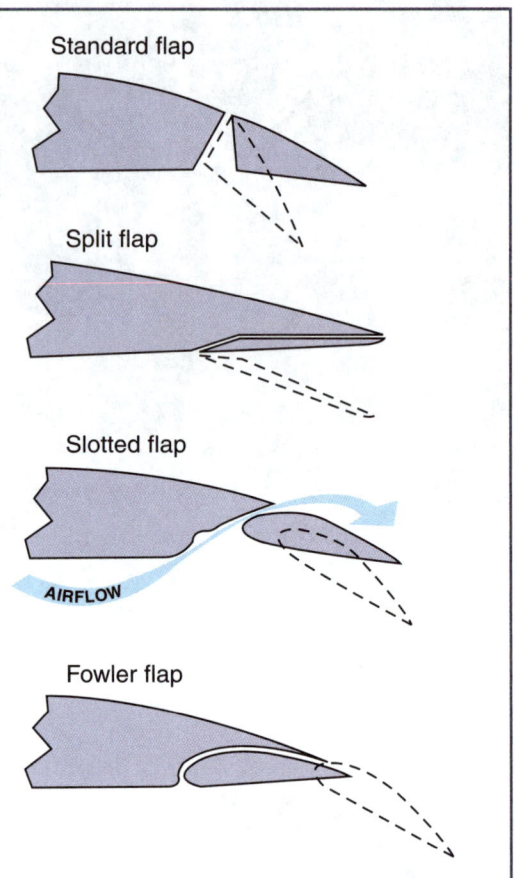

Winglets

Airliners also have to be efficient. After all, fuel is expensive, and if airliners burn too much fuel in order to go fast, the airlines have to raise the price of tickets, which will cost them customers. So designers of airliners (and some business jets) sometimes add certain things to the wings to reduce drag, since an airplane with less drag needs less power (thrust) to force it through the air, which means it will use less fuel.

Some airliners, for example, have **winglets**, or small vertical fins, on the tips of their wings. What do these devices do? Well, remember how the movement of a plane through the air, like the movement of a boat through the water, creates a turbulent wake? One of the places where a plane's wake is most violent is behind its wing tips. Since air and objects try to move to low pressure areas, the high pressure air under the wing wants to move to the low pressure area on top of the wing. This creates a swirl of air around the tip of the wing. As this swirling air separates from the airplane at the wingtip, it's turns into a horizontal tornado. No kidding! NASA did some flight research at its Dryden Flight Research Center with wingtip **vortices**, as these tornadoes of air are called, and found that the vortices were so powerful, they could flip a small jet flying behind the airliner upside down!

NASA photo

But these tornadoes of air cause a LOT of drag. You might think that adding something to a plane's wing would give it more drag. But **winglets** help reduce wingtip vortices and their drag by breaking up the air coming off the wingtip. This makes the wing more efficient.

Build Your Own Wings

The teenagers in this photo are learning how to build their own airplane wings through the EAA Aviation Foundation's Air Academy program. The EAA Air Academy consists of week-long residence camps for youth ages 12-18, held at the Experimental Aircraft Association's headquarters in Oshkosh, Wisconsin. In addition to a variety of recreational activities, participants learn about building wings and airplanes, design, build and fly their own kites, hot air balloons, and balsa gliders, fly control-line models, work with flight simulators, and even get a flight in an actual airplane (if weather conditions permit). Older participants also get ground school instruction toward an actual pilot's license. For more information, contact the EAA Resident Education Department at 888-322-3299 or by email at education@eaa.org.

Photo courtesy of EAA

Real Life Profile: Allison Turner
Airline Captain, ComAir Airlines, Cincinnati, OH

Allison Turner always thought it would be fun to fly but thought it would be too hard. She was an adult before she met a couple of pilots and realized they were just average people. "If they could do it," she says," I figured I could do it."

Turner worked as a flight instructor before being hired by ComAir. "You sure don't make much money as a flight instructor, but it's fun, and it helps you build time," she says. Captain Turner now has more than 10,000 flight hours and flies Regional Jets.

"Flying for an airline's not for everyone," she says. "It's like driving a car 12-14 hours a day with only a few stops for fuel and food. But I really DO like the flying. And it's flexible hours, not an 8-to-5 job."

"If I had it to do again, I'd have tried flying as a teenager," she says, "to see if I really liked it. After all, you can learn to fly before you learn to drive."

Cargo Wings

Cargo planes are the pick-up trucks of the aviation world. They're not fast, smooth, or exciting-looking. But they are very useful and perform many important — and exciting — jobs. Cargo planes transport jeeps, troops and parachuters, as well as military, medical and other supplies all around the world. Some cargo planes transport even more exotic items, such as whales, elephants or dead bodies. A cargo plane going into an airport in Ohio once couldn't get its gear to come down and had to "belly land" with a full load of poisonous snakes from Africa. Talk about exciting jobs!

What does it take to make an airplane that can do these jobs? Think about what a cargo plane's main challenge is. A cargo plane has to be stable and has to carry a lot of weight. This means most cargo planes need big, thick wings with rounded leading edges that generate a lot of lift. A lot of cargo planes have straight wings, not swept wings, because they don't need to go fast. They just need to carry a lot.

There are also some jet cargo planes that have swept wings. Some Boeing 747s, for example, carry only cargo — as much as a *quarter million pounds* of it! A B-52 bomber is also a kind of cargo plane — it has to carry a heavy load of bombs. But the B-52 also has to move fast enough not to get shot down. So the B-52 was designed with a very big and long swept wing so it could go fast and yet still create enough lift to get the airplane off the ground. The problem with a wing that long is that there's no way to keep it rigid. It will flex (move up and down) a lot. So the B-52 has little wheels under its wingtips to keep the wingtips from scraping on the ground when it's taking off and landing.

Many military cargo planes not only have to carry a lot, they also have to be able to get in and out of short airstrips. So they have to combine cargo and STOL (Short Take-Off and Landing) wing designs. This C-17, for example, not only has HUGE engines, it has leading edge slats and big slotted flaps that extend behind the engines on the wings. The engine exhaust blows through the flap slot and over the flap, creating even more lift. This lets the airplane descend at a steeper angle and land in a shorter distance.

Photos courtesy of The Boeing Company

Look-down view of a C-17 wing.

Cross-section of a C-17 wing, showing airfoil.

C-17

Photo courtesy of Cessna Aircraft Company

This Cessna Caravan plane is built specifically to carry cargo. This means that it's more important for it to be sturdy than fast. Its wings are straight, high-lift wings and are supported by struts, which makes them stronger. Its gear is also "fixed," which saves the weight and room that a gear retraction system would need.

NASA photo

Special Cargo: NASA's Shuttle Carrier Aircraft

Question: How do you transport cargo that's bigger than the inside of any cargo plane?

Answer: You strap it on the OUTSIDE of a cargo plane!

When the Space Shuttle lands at Edwards Air Force Base in California (where NASA's Dryden Flight Research Center is located), it's put on the back of this special Boeing 747 to ferry it back to the Kennedy Space Flight Center in Florida. In order for it to carry the weight of the Shuttle, a lot of the 747's interior, such as seats and padding, is taken out to make it as light as possible. Because the Shuttle blocks the vertical tail of the 747, two extra vertical fins were also added to the outside edges of the jet's horizontal stabilizer so it would still be controllable, even with this bulky burden on its back.

Unusual Cargo — NASA's B-52 Mothership

One of the world's most unusual cargo planes is NASA's B-52 "Mothership." It's a B-52 bomber, but it doesn't carry bombs. It carries airplanes. Not inside, but outside, on a special pod under its right wing. Why? Because some experimental planes don't have engines or don't carry much fuel (especially rocket planes). So the B-52 is used to carry these planes up to a high altitude and drop-launch them. The planes then only have to glide or fly back to a landing. The B-52 has carried many different test vehicles, including the X-15, NASA's lifting body planes and the X-38 research spacecraft. (If you want to know more about these amazing research airplanes, read the section on "Space Wings.")

NASA photos

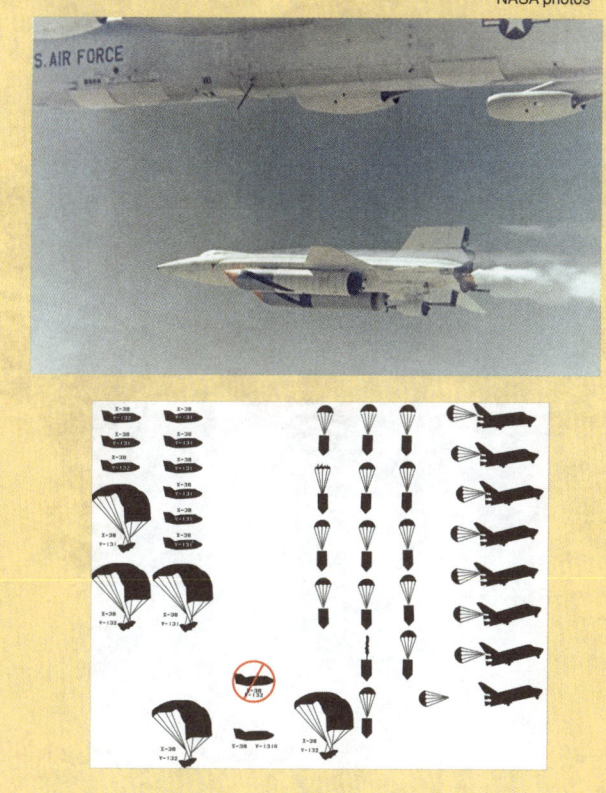

Aerobatic Wings

What if you wanted to be a famous air show pilot and do loops, spins, snap rolls and other rough-and-tumble maneuvers in front of thousands of people? What kind of airplane would you need? Obviously, you'd need a plane that would turn and maneuver easily. But what wings help a plane do that?

One thing to remember is that turning sharply (like the car on a curvy road or a roller coaster) creates high "G," or gravity, forces. So the wing of an aerobatic plane needs to be strong enough not to break when it's pulling 6 or 7 times the airplane's weight in a turn. This is why a lot of aerobatic planes are biplanes. Strut and wire-braced wings give them a lot of strength, which means the wing itself can be lighter. Having two wings also lets each wing be shorter, which helps the plane roll faster.

But biplanes create a lot of drag (re-read the section on "Drag" for more on this). New composite materials now allow designers to build aerobatic wings strong and light enough that they can build single-wing aerobatic planes. The top-performing aerobatic planes today are **monoplanes** (which means they have one wing instead of an upper and lower wing, like a **biplane**).

Another thing that helps a plane turn sharply is making those strong wings lightly **loaded**. For a refresher on wing loading, re-read the "Wings" section. Civilian aerobatic planes tend to be relatively lightweight, so their wings don't have to create a lot of lift to support their weight. With a lightly loaded wing, the plane doesn't need to build

Photo courtesy of EAA

Pitts Biplane

Look-down view of a Pitts biplane wing.

Cross-section of a Pitts biplane wing, showing airfoil.

up as much speed before it can safely pull a "high-G" turn. It will still have enough lift to fly through the maneuver at slow speeds, so it can make tighter turns. If the wing and plane are light, it also means the engine has "extra" thrust available to make the plane do things normal planes can't do — like climb straight up in the air.

Aerobatic planes also need to be less stable than many other kinds of planes. Remember in the Stability section, when we talked about wing **dihedral**? Having the wings mounted at an upward angle from the fuselage (dihedral) helps a plane stay right side up. Designers say this means the plane has **positive stability**. But an aerobatic pilot doesn't WANT to keep the wings right side up. You don't want to have to fight the plane to get it to roll upside down. For this reason, aerobatic wings usually have **neutral stability**, which means that the wings have less of an upward angle from the fuselage. This helps the plane go wherever the pilot points it. But this makes aerobatic planes harder to fly straight and level.

Photo courtesy of EAA

Symmetrical Wings

Aerobatic planes spend a lot of time UPSIDE DOWN. What does this do to plane's wing and the lift it can create? (Think it through. The curve on the top side of the wing makes air move faster across that surface, which creates lower pressure there, which pulls the wing in that direction. So if the top, curved side of the wing is facing the *ground* when the plane is upside down ... Right. It's a problem.) If an aerobatic plane has a normal wing with a curved top and flat bottom, its lift is pulling it toward the ground when it's upside down. That's not what pilots want! So many newer aerobatic planes have **symmetrical wings** — that is, they're curved on both the top and the bottom.

But if the wings are curved on both sides, the air isn't really going any faster on the top than the bottom. So how does a pilot create lift? By using **angle of attack**. Remember how raising an airplane's angle of attack makes the wing act as if it's got a bigger curve in the wing? Aerobatic pilots can point the nose of the plane up above the plane's flight path — whether the plane is right side up or upside down — and create the lift they need to fly. With symmetrical wings, at least they're not fighting the wing.

Photo courtesy of Wayne Handley

Wayne Handley's Oracle Turbo Raven

This neat-looking "bat-plane," which was flown by aerobatic champion and air show pilot Wayne Handley, was one of the highest-performance aerobatic planes ever to fly on the air show circuit. In January 1999, it set an all-time climb record for a propeller airplane, beating records held by Chuck Yeager (of X-1 fame) and the pilot of a 7-time national champion air racing plane.

What was this plane's secret? It had a 750 horsepower turboprop engine. Most aerobatic planes have only 200 - 300 horsepower piston engines. (Read the section on "Engines" to find out more about the differences between turboprop and piston engines.)

The Turbo Raven's powerful engine put out more thrust, in pounds, than the airplane weighed! This meant that the Oracle Turbo Raven could climb straight up in the air without a lot of trouble!

Real Life Profile: Patty Wagstaff
National Aerobatic Champion, Air Show Pilot
St. Augustine, FL

Patty Wagstaff didn't start flying until she was an adult. But within five years of getting her pilot's license, she was one of the top aerobatic pilots in the world. She has won three national aerobatic championships and is one of the top air show performers in the country.

"I love all kinds of flying," she says, "but I always want to get back to aerobatics. Nothing compares to the feeling of tumbling, floating and dancing through the air."

Although she never planned a career in flying, Wagstaff says that working in aviation or aerospace is "the most exciting challenging career you can have." She also says that it's easier than people think to get involved or find out more about it. "Just go to a small, local airport, anywhere in the country," she says. "You'll find lots of encouraging, friendly faces there."

NASA photo

Fighters

What if your mission isn't an air show, but a dogfight over enemy territory? Military fighters are another kind of aerobatic plane, but they aren't very light. They have to carry a lot of ammunition, weapons, and equipment. This means that they have to have a beefy structure to keep from breaking in high-G maneuvers. Because they're heavy, fighters also need to create a lot of lift. But they can't use high-lift wings, because they need to be fast and maneuverable.

If you look at most modern fighters, you'll see that most of them have fast wings (thin, short, and swept back), so they can fly fast. They get enough lift to carry their heavy weight by using a lot of thrust and flying very quickly. This is why military jet fighters have HUGE engines, usually with **afterburners**. (To learn more about afterburners, read the section on jet engines.)

Many fighters are now built to be *unstable*, because that makes them really maneuverable. An unstable airplane doesn't just keep turning in whatever direction you point it. It doesn't want to stay level at all. Before the invention of flight computers, it would have been very difficult for a pilot to fly an unstable airplane. But today, computers can let pilots fly really unstable designs like the F-16 and F-117A and perform amazing maneuvers with them.

The F-18 "Hornet" (above) also has some handy tricks to make it more maneuverable. It has leading edge slats and trailing edge flaps that extend automatically when the plane's computer senses that it needs more lift. So if the pilot is pulling a tight maneuver that slows the plane down, the plane's computer will "decide" it needs more lift and extend either the slats or the flaps, or both, however far the computer thinks they need to be extended to make enough lift.

NASA photo

NASA's HiMAT

Have you ever flown a radio-controlled airplane? Well, THIS radio-controlled airplane would blow the socks off any other RC plane out there! It was a NASA research plane called the "HiMAT," which stands for "Highly Maneuverable Aircraft Technology," and it was powered by an afterburning jet engine. Engineers at Dryden used it to look at ways they could make an airplane more maneuverable, or aerobatic. The HiMAT had a forward **canard**, **winglets**, and sharply **swept wings**. The wings were made of graphite and fiberglass, which made them very stiff and strong. The HiMAT's wings were also built to automatically flex downward when the plane was pulling a lot of "Gs," giving the wings a greater curve, or **camber**. When the wings flexed, it made the wings able to create more lift. This helped the HiMAT keep flying even when the plane was flying slower in tight, "high-G" turns

Flexible Wings

Not all wings are solid structures. Since the invention of the kite, people have also designed and built wings made of fabric. In the 1500s, the artist and inventor Leonardo da Vinci designed a hang glider that, four centuries later, became the inspiration for the "Batman" cartoon figure. Da Vinci never tested his design, but today many people fly hang gliders. To fly a hang glider, the pilot "hangs" beneath what is basically a giant kite and glides down from a hilltop or cliff.

Hang gliders are a type of wing. So are modern, rectangle-shaped parachutes. NASA has even experimented with the use of flexible fabric or inflatable wings to help bring spacecraft safely back to Earth.

The X-38, for example, was designed as a research vehicle that might lead to a kind of "lifeboat" spacecraft for astronauts on the International Space Station. If such a spacecraft ever had to be used, its computer autopilot would steer it back down into the Earth's atmosphere, so injured astronauts could get back home without having to fly the spacecraft themselves. Once it got close to the ground, it would deploy this controllable parachute to bring it down to a gentle landing. The X-38's parachute is really a flexible airfoil that can be controlled, just like the rectangular-shaped parachutes skydivers use. How?

Remember how a pilot pulls a plane's wing up at an angle to create more lift in an airplane? The X-38's parachute works the same way — pull down on the back edge of the parachute, and the front edge will go up. This creates more lift and slows the X-38 down. Pull the front edge down and the X-38 will descend at a steeper angle and speed up. The parachute uses the same basic technique as a Flying Wing to turn. (You can read more about the Flying Wing on page 79.) To turn right with a steerable parachute, you pull down on strings connected to the back, right-hand edge of the chute. Pulling the back edge of the chute down creates drag on that side. That extra drag pulls the right side of the parachute back, making the parachute turn right. If you pulled the back edge of the parachute's left side down, the parachute would turn left.

NASA photo

X-38 Parafoil

Look-down view of the X-38 Parafoil wing.

Cross-section of the X-38 Parafoil wing, showing airfoil.

The Paresev

At the beginning of the space program, NASA experimented with an unusual system for bringing the Gemini space capsules back to Earth. Some researchers thought a steerable, inflatable wing might allow the astronauts to steer the capsule back to a safe landing on land, instead of splashing down in the ocean. To see if the concept would work, a small paraglider called the Paresev was built and flight tested at the Dryden Flight Research Center. Two different flexible wings were tested on the Paresev, which resembled a hang glider attached to a 3-wheeled dune buggy. The craft wasn't very stable, and NASA eventually gave up on the idea. But the better parachutes available today have made NASA look at this general idea again for the X-38.

NASA photo

Photo by Ines Roberts

Paragliding vs. Parachuting

Paragliders use flexible wings that are very much like parachutes but are designed for a different mission. A parachute is designed to slow a skydiver's (or spacecraft's) descent. To do this, a parachute has withstand the shock of a sudden opening and open gently enough not to hurt its cargo. It then has to have enough lift to bring that cargo down to a safe and gentle landing.

A paraglider is also a flexible airfoil that inflates as air flows in between its top and bottom layers, but it's sole design goal is to create as much lift as possible. Paraglider pilots start with their chutes open behind them and the chutes inflate slowly as the pilots run down a slope. By the time a paraglider pilot jumps off the hillside, the chute is inflated. All it has to do is create as much lift as possible. If paraglider pilots can find rising air, they can stay up in the air and soar like a hang glider pilot — flying in the air without the solid tubes and framework hang gliders need. But the bigger and more lightweight paragliders can't withstand high winds or "G" forces.

Ultralights

What would happen if you put an engine on a hang glider? You'd get an ultralight. Ultralights are kind of a cross between a hang glider and an airplane. They're extremely lightweight, with very small engines. A lot of times, ultralights are little more than a pilot seat hanging beneath a fabric wing. They don't go fast, and they don't fly well in any kind of windy weather. But ultralights are good planes to take sightseeing, low and slow.

Photo courtesy of EAA

Space Wings

What if you wanted to build a plane that could travel outside the atmosphere? What kind of wings would it have to have? If it were only going to travel in space, it wouldn't have to have wings at all. (Look at the early space capsule shapes!) But if you wanted it to be able to fly back into the Earth's atmosphere and land like an airplane, your spaceplane would need a way of creating at least some lift.

The problem is that normal airplane wings couldn't survive a re-entry into the atmosphere from space. Why? Spacecraft move incredibly fast in space, because there are no air molecules to offer any resistance to forward movement. They also need a lot of speed to maintain orbit. When spacecraft come back into the Earth's atmosphere, they're still flying at speeds as high as 25 times the speed of sound (around 18,000 miles an hour). When something is moving that fast through the atmosphere, all those air molecules flying over its wings create a lot of friction. If you've ever skidded your leg across a gym floor, you know that friction creates a lot of heat. The same is true with airplane wings. The heat caused by the friction of air molecules at Mach 5, 10, 15 or 20 is so high that most wings would melt off the plane!

So if you look at the Space Shuttle, you'll notice that the wings are very thick, with blunt, rounded leading edges. Thick wings with thick, blunt leading edges heat up more slowly than thin wings, just as a thick piece of toast takes longer to heat up than a thin one does. The Shuttle wings are also covered with insulating tiles to protect them from the heat of re-entry and high-speed flight.

The Space Shuttle is not the only kind of space wing NASA has, however. The X-15 was a research plane from the 1960s that flew to the edge of space and more than six times the speed of sound (about 4,000 miles per hour). Its wings weren't as thick as those on the Space Shuttle, because the X-15 still flew a lot slower than the Shuttle does. NASA also built and flew some really weird planes called lifting bodies that had no wings at all!

The Space Shuttle

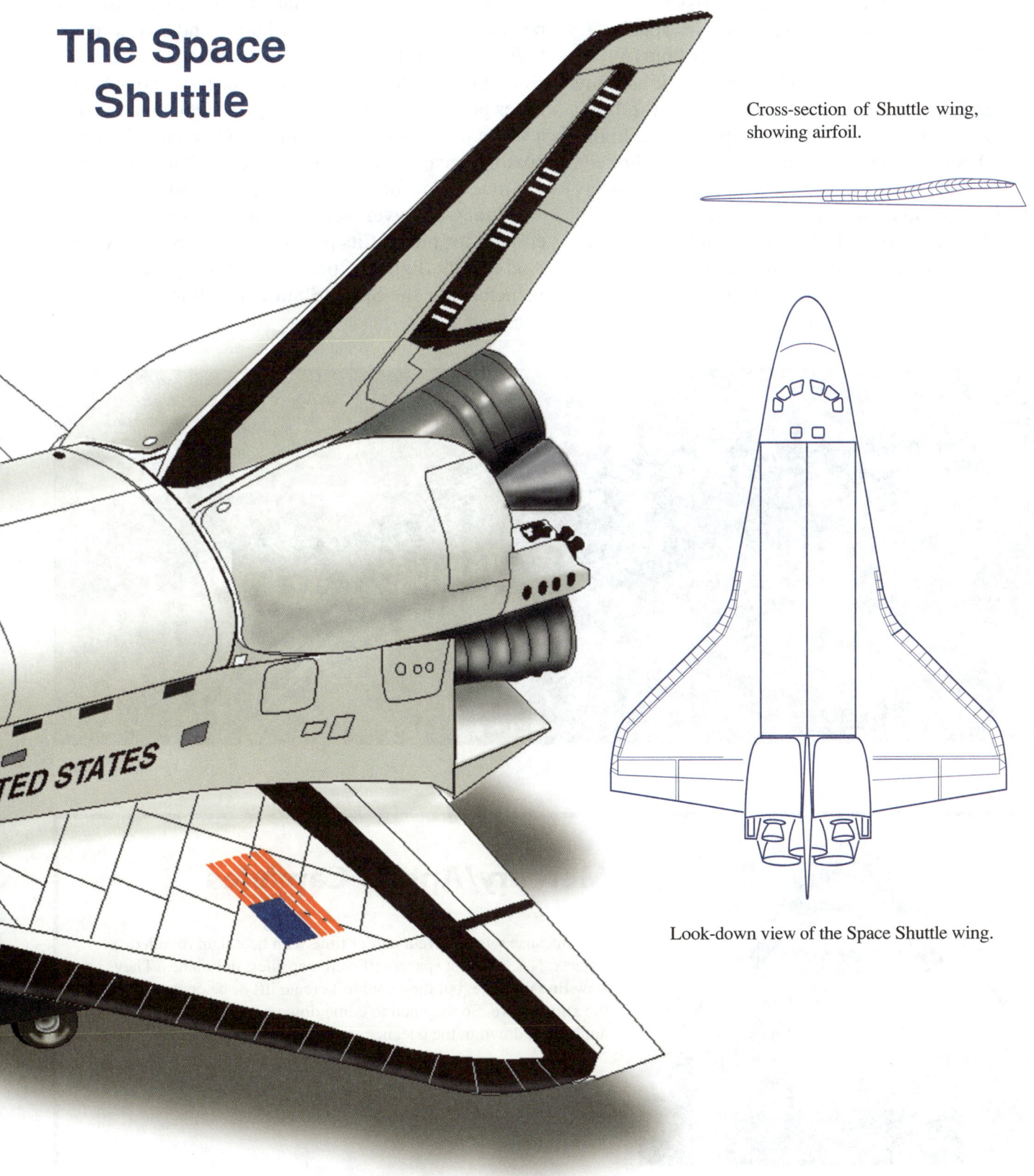

Cross-section of Shuttle wing, showing airfoil.

Look-down view of the Space Shuttle wing.

X-15

The X-15 was a rocket plane that was built to research flight at hypersonic speeds — or speeds above Mach 5 (or about 3,000 miles per hour). Because it was built for such high speeds, it had tiny little wings. It didn't need to create a lot of lift, but it had to withstand very high temperatures — as high as 1,200 degrees! Twelve hundred degrees is hotter than the heat coming out the engine of a modern day fighter plane. So although the X-15 had thinner wings than the Space Shuttle, they still had rounded front edges so they would resist heat better. Its wings were also built out of a weird, heat-resistant metal mixture called "Inconel X."

The X-15 flew faster than any plane that has ever been built except the Space Shuttle, and it flew as high as 350,000 feet — 70 miles above the Earth! But on its fastest flights, above Mach 6 (about 4,000 miles per hour), the engineers painted the plane with a white heat-resistant coating. They had to add the coating because the friction of going that fast created too much heat for even Inconel X to stand.

The X-15 never went into orbit, but it flew high enough for most of its pilots to earn astronaut wings. And its 199 flights helped make other space vehicles, like the Space Shuttle, possible.

Painting by Stan Stokes

Mercury/Apollo Capsules

Because wings have a harder time with heat than rounded objects, NASA's first spacecraft were capsules, not planes. They flew fine in space, but they couldn't create lift or be controlled in the atmosphere. So they had to come down under big parachutes and splash down in the ocean.

Flying Bathtubs

NASA photo

These weird-looking flying machines were built to see if it was possible to build something without wings that could still fly. Something without wings was ideal for withstanding the heat of re-entering the Earth's atmosphere. But to be flown back to a landing, a spacecraft has to be able to create lift. The idea of these "lifting body" planes was to use their rounded bodies to create that lift. Air passing over their curved bodies would speed up, creating lift.

Few people believed that this bizarre shape would actually fly. To prove that it would, a small group of engineers at NASA's Dryden Flight Research Center built a lifting body out of plywood and towed it behind a souped-up Pontiac convertible. The official name of the stubby plywood plane was the "M2-F1," although many people called it the "Flying Bathtub" because of its shape. It looked funny, but it worked.

Today, designers are looking at lifting body designs again. The X-38 (a potential rescue craft for future astronauts on the Space Station) is a lifting body design. (You can read more about the X-38 in the section on "Flexible Wings.") The spacecraft that replaces the Space Shuttle may also be a lifting body.

NASA photo

The Lunar Module

What if a plane is going to operate only in space? That was the case with the Lunar Module that landed astronauts on the moon. It didn't need to create any lift, so it didn't need any wings or even a lifting body shape. But it still needed to be controlled. How can you do that without wings or control surfaces? Read the section on "Space Controls" to find out!

NASA photo

Helicopter Wings

If wings are what create the lift to let an aircraft fly, how do helicopters fly? They don't have any wings! The answer is that a helicopter may not LOOK like it has wings, but it actually does. Its rotor blades — the blades that rotate above the helicopter — are each shaped like a thin, long, flexible wing. As they rotate around, air flows over them and creates lift. This is what lets a helicopter fly. A helicopter can also fly straight up, because its turning rotor blades don't need forward movement to have air going over them.

All of the blades (helicopters usually have 2 or 4 blades) can also tilt together — forward, back, and sideways. This is what makes the helicopter turn. If the rotor blades are parallel with the ground, they are pushing **thrust** straight toward the ground and creating **lift** straight up. So the helicopter moves straight up. If the rotors are tilted forward, they are pushing air back and down and lift up and forward, so the helicopter will move forward. If the rotors are tilted back, they are pushing air forward and lift back, so the helicopter will move backward.

If you've ever wound up the propeller of a rubber-band-powered balsa wood model and let go of the plane accidentally while still holding on to the propeller, you probably discovered that a spinning rotor makes the object it's attached to spin quite quickly in the opposite direction. The same is true with helicopters. If they only had a rotor above the fuselage, the fuselage would spin uncontrollably in the opposite direction as the rotors were turning. That's why helicopters have a vertical **tail rotor**, as well. The tail rotor sends thrust in the opposite direction to the way the fuselage wants to spin, stabilizing the helicopter.

Bell 206L Long Ranger

Photo courtesy of Bell Helicopter Textron

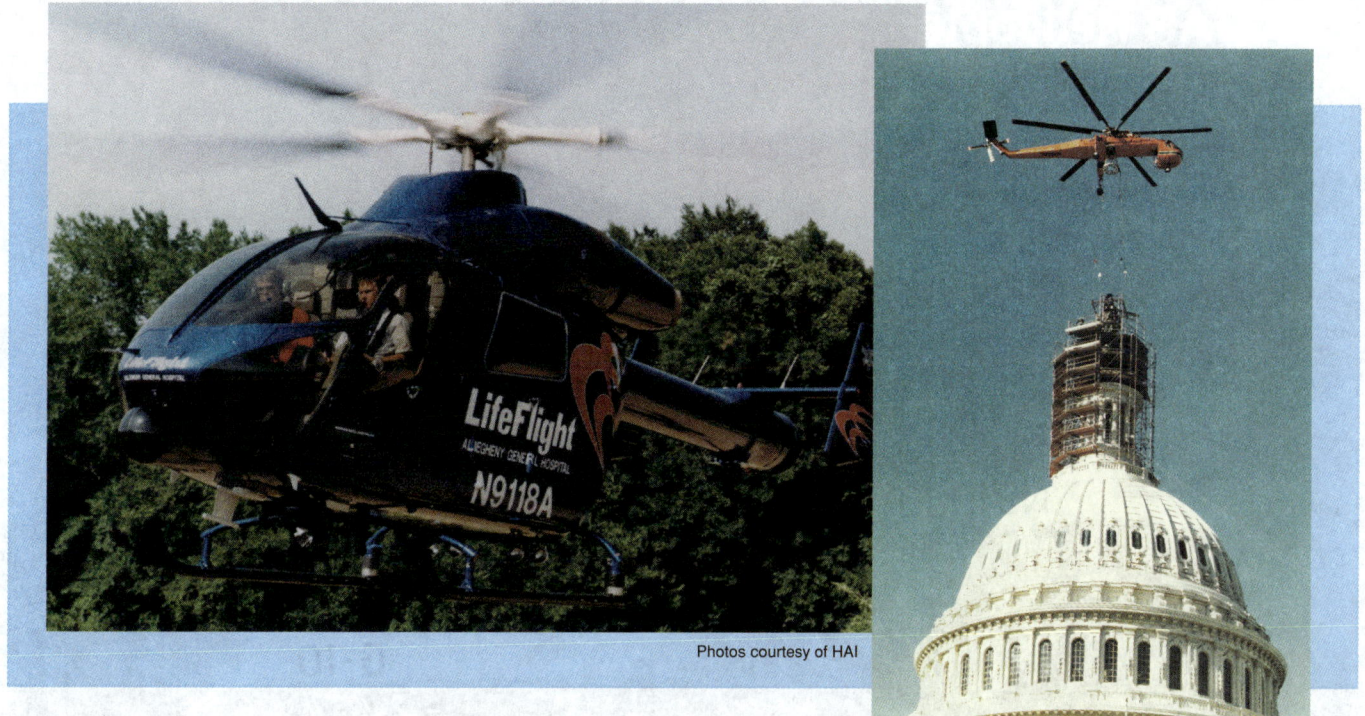

Photos courtesy of HAI

Because helicopters can fly straight up, sideways and backwards, and stay perfectly still in one spot in the air, they can do all sorts of jobs. They can land on highways and in school yards to take injured people to the hospital. They can help firefighters get equipment into remote places to fight forest fires. They can carry Christmas trees out of the forest and rescue stranded hikers on the sides of mountains. They can land on small oil rigs in the middle of the ocean, and they also let movie directors get all sorts of difficult camera shots.

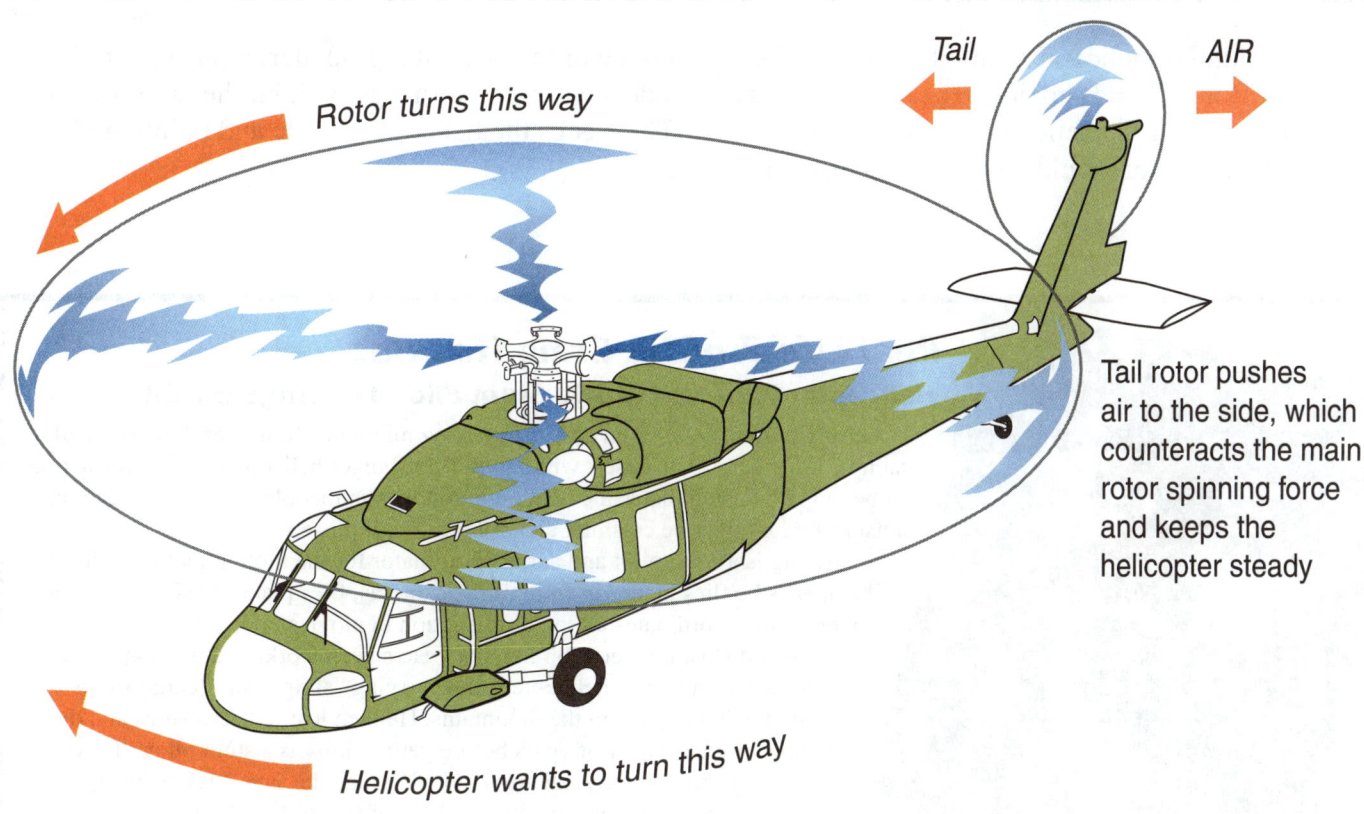

NOTAR Helicopter

Photo courtesy of HAI

A new kind of helicopter, called a "Notar," for "NO TAil Rotor," sends engine exhaust out of slots in the tail boom of the helicopter to do the same thing that a tail rotor would do. It's like a using a jet on the tail instead of a propeller to push the tail sideways (if the thrust goes right, the tail goes left). This keeps the helicopter stable and pointing straight ahead.

Real Life Profile: Craig Hosking
Helicopter Pilot and Movie Stunt Pilot, Los Angeles, CA

On any particular work day, Craig Hosking might be chasing Mel Gibson and Danny Glover across the desert with his Bell JetRanger helicopter to film the action. Or he might be using that same helicopter to tow stuntpeople across the ocean on Jetskis. Or he might be crashing an airplane...on purpose.

Hosking is a stunt pilot and aerial coordinator for the motion picture industry. That means he flies planes in front of the cameras, flies planes CARRYING the cameras, and coordinates all the flying action in movies.

How did Hosking get a job like that? He's been working at it a long time. He started working as a helicopter pilot carrying "sling loads"(cargo slung beneath the helicopter) in the mountains. He then learned aerobatics and did air shows for a number of years before getting jobs as a stunt pilot. "I love everything about flying, and any kind of flying," he says. "It lets me operate cool machines and have an amazing kind of freedom and fun."

Make Your Own Helicopter!

Want to see for yourself how a helicopter makes lift? Try making your own paper helicopter! (Template for the helicopter is on page 160)

1. Trace the template onto a piece of paper. You can try different kinds of papers — construction paper, copy or computer paper, notebook paper — and see how the paper weight affects how the helicopter flies.

2. Cut along the solid lines of the template and fold along the dotted lines. The propeller blades should be folded in opposite directions. X and Y fold toward the center, and Z is folded up to give the body rigidity and a lower center of gravity.

3. Take the helicopter in one hand and an unfolded piece of paper in the other. Drop them both at the same time. Which one falls faster? (Answer: The paper does, because it's not creating lift. The only force on it is gravity. If you wad up the paper, it will fall even faster, because it has less surface area exposed to offer resistance to the air molecules between it and the ground.)

Real Life Profile: Bonnie Wilkens
Helicopter Firefighter Pilot, AgRotors, Inc.
Fairfield, PA

Bonnie Wilkens does many types of jobs with the helicopters she flies. But her favorite type of work is fighting forest fires.

Wilkens works all over in the United States during fire season – wherever the fires are. One of the things she does is carry firefighters in close to the fires. If she can land, she drops them off. If there's no landing spot, they rappel out of the helicopter while she hovers above the trees. She'll then go pick up a "bambi bucket," which she carries on a long line beneath the helicopter. She picks up water from lakes or ponds in the bucket and then dumps it on specific "hot spots" in the fire.

"I never would have picked this out of a career book," she says, "but I love it. Fighting fires is hard work, but it's exciting. It's also productive, and when you're fighting fires, you're really the good guy. I like that."

Weird Wings

Sometimes designers come up with really weird wing designs in an effort to make planes perform better or do jobs they couldn't do before. Many of these designs are tested at NASA's Dryden Flight Research Center in California. Here are just a few of them.

Forward Swept Wing

This is the X-29. It was a research plane built to test new designs, including a forward swept wing. In theory, designers thought a forward swept wing would reduce drag at high speeds just like a conventional swept wing. But a forward swept wing was also supposed to fly better at slower speeds and high **angles of attack** (when the plane's nose is pointing very high above the plane's flight path).

The problem is that a forward swept wing has to be a lot stronger in order not to twist and break. You can see this for yourself by holding your arm straight out of the family car window while the car is travelling fairly fast. Now try swinging your arm forward and holding it there. It's a lot harder, isn't it? It wasn't until designers figured out how to use graphite/fiberglass composite materials to build a wing that they could make a wing strong enough for this design to work.

The X-29 flew very well. The wing had less drag than a typical straight wing, and it flew better at high angles of attack than a conventional swept wing. This may lead designers to build a production plane with a forward-swept wing some day. The X-29 also tested how unstable a plane could be and still be controllable with flight control computers. The X-29 was so unstable that if its three flight computers had all failed, it would have gone out of control in less than a second. So the computers had to be VERY reliable! But it helped engineers learn more about designing an unstable, computer-controlled airplane.

NASA photo

Changeable Wings

One of the the problems in trying to make high-speed wings is that the wings also have to work at slower speeds in order for the airplane to take off and land. Airliner wings solve this problem by extending slats and flaps to make the wing fly better at slow speeds. But that's not the only way designers have found to give an airplane two different kinds of wings in one.

Oblique Wing

A more unusual approach to designing two wings in one was called the **oblique wing**, and it was tested on a plane called the AD-1.

The AD-1 had a wing that could pivot, or swing around, at its center point. For take off, landing, and slow-speed flight, the wing was kept in a straight out, "unswept," position. But at high speeds, the wing could be swung around so that one end of the wing pointed forward, toward the nose of the plane, and the other end of the wing trailed behind, pointing more toward the tail.

Having the wing pointing forward created a lot less drag. Of course, when the wing was positioned like that, it also created less lift, since air wasn't flowing straight over the wing. But at high speeds, wings don't need to be as efficient at making lift. So the design was able to work.

NASA photo

NASA photo

Swing-Wing

Another way of creating two different wings in one is called a "swing-wing." The first plane to use this was the X-5 — an experimental research plane flown at Dryden in the early 1950s. An F-14 fighter also has this kind of wing. A swing wing can be positioned straight out for take off, landing, and slow flight. But it can then swing backward into a swept position for high-speed flight. This gives it much less drag. When the plane comes back in to land, the wing is brought forward again into a straight out position.

Mission Adaptive Wing

Another type of changeable wing, called a **Mission Adaptive Wing** actually changed its curve (or **camber**) in flight. The F-111 fighter that tested the wing used internal controls to flex the wing and change its camber for different types of flight. It flexed the wing so the wing had a big curve for slow flight, and it flexed it back to a more streamlined curve for high-speed flight.

NASA photo

Lopsided Wing

This really weird-looking airplane is called the *Boomerang*. It was designed by Burt Rutan — the same person who designed the *Voyager* (see the section on long-range wings). It's got a lopsided design because Rutan wanted to keep its engines close together. Most conventional 2-engine (or "twin") airplanes have an engine on each side of the fuselage. The problem with this design is that if one engine fails, the plane's thrust becomes lopsided — the only working engine is out on one wing, which makes the plane want to turn the other way. By making the *plane* lopsided, Rutan made the two engines on the Boomerang close together. So if one engine fails, the remaining engine (and thrust) is still pretty close to the center of the airplane, keeping it from **yawing**, or turning, to one side. This makes the airplane safer.

NASA photo

Photo courtesy of EAA

Tilt-Rotor

This tilt-rotor design is for people who can't decide whether they want a helicopter or a plane. It's a mix of both. It's engines can tilt up, so they look and act like helicopter rotors. Or they can tilt back down level with the wing, so they act like propellers. This means the tilt-rotor can take off vertically, like a helicopter, and then turn into an airplane in flight. The pilot just hits a switch that lowers the rotors down until they are level with the wing. This tilt-rotor can go from hovering like a helicopter with no forward movement to flying forward as an airplane at almost 280 miles per hour in only 22 seconds!

Control Surfaces

Another important part of an airplane's design that affects the kind of job it can do is the kind of **control surfaces** the plane uses. Most airplanes are controlled with ailerons, rudders, and elevators.

Ailerons are moveable surfaces on the back edge of the wing that control an airplane's roll (how the wings move up and down). The **rudder** is a moveable surface on the plane's vertical tail that controls its yaw (how the tail moves left and right). The **elevators** are moveable surfaces on the horizontal tail of the airplane that control its pitch (how the nose moves up and down). Go back and read the section on "Control" if you need a refresher on how these surfaces work.

Aerobatic Controls

Not all ailerons, rudders and elevators are alike. If you wanted to build a plane that was going to perform all sorts of wild maneuvers, for example, you'd need different kinds of control surfaces than if you wanted a docile plane that was going to stay straight and level and only fly business trips.

Aerobatic pilots and fighter pilots both need control surfaces that respond very fast and very well. How would you make surfaces that could do that? Well, for one thing, you would make all the surfaces very BIG. A big surface is going to deflect more air, which is going to make the airplane turn more quickly.

Look at a lot of aerobatic biplanes, and you'll see they have double sets of ailerons — on both the top and bottom wings. This gives these planes twice as much aileron power, so they roll very quickly.

Photo courtesy of EAA

Balanced Controls

Aerobatic planes also need controls that are easy to move, even in high-G maneuvers when the airplane and its control surfaces are heavier than normal. So designers do different things to help balance and move the control surfaces.

Because the hinge point of this aileron is back from its leading edge a little, the front part sticks up above the wing when the aileron is deflected down, and sticks down when the aileron is deflected up. What does this do? Think about it. Say the pilot wants to turn left. The right aileron needs to go down and the left one needs to go up. As the right aileron goes down, the front part of it will stick up above the wing. The air coming over the wing will hit the underside of this piece, helping to force the aileron down even more. On the left wing, the opposite thing is taking place. As the aileron comes up,

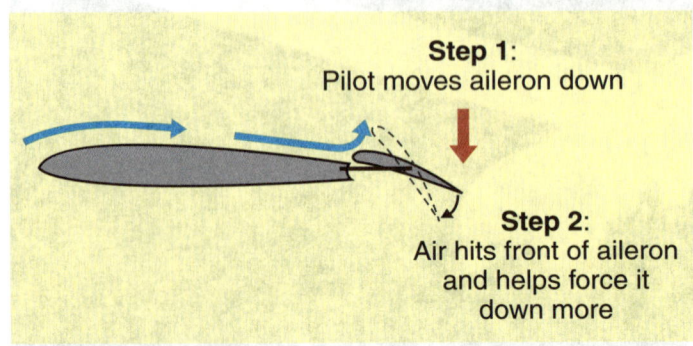

Step 1: Pilot moves aileron down

Step 2: Air hits front of aileron and helps force it down more

the front part of it sticks out below the wing. The airstream will hit the front side of that piece, helping to force the aileron up even more. As a result, the pilot needs to use a lot less force to move the ailerons and make the plane roll. This same technique can also be used on a plane's elevators.

Spades

Another way pilots make ailerons easier to move is by adding something called **spades** to the underside of the ailerons. A spade is an angled, "L-shaped" piece of metal that hangs below the aileron. The lower portion of the "L" is a wide, flat surface, which is why it's called a spade. When the pilot moves the aileron up, that moves the spade so that the *front* surface of the spade is facing into the airstream. The air pushes on the spade, which pushes the aileron up even further. If the pilot moves the aileron down, it puts the *back* surface of the spade into the airstream. The air pushing on the back side of the spade helps pull the aileron down even further. This means that the pilot doesn't have to pull as hard on the control stick to get the plane to roll.

A similar kind of device is sometimes used on a plane's elevator, as well.

Aerobatic plane showing spades below wing.

Spoilers

Sometimes, high performance controls are used to make an airplane slow down or descend quickly. A glider, for example, has a wing that's very good at creating lift. It's SO good, in fact, that it can be hard to get it to STOP creating lift when you want to land. And since a glider has no engine, it only gets one try at making the runway. So gliders have **spoilers** that can be raised vertically from the top of the wing. When the spoilers come out, they "spoil" the smooth air flow over the wing. That makes the wing stop making lift, which lets the glider descend and land quickly. Airliners, many jet fighters, and some other high-performance planes also have spoilers they can raise on their wings to help them descend or slow down quickly.

Glider with spoilers deployed above wing.

Speed Brakes

Another way to get an airplane to descend quickly without gaining speed or just slow down is to increase the amount of drag on the airplane. Think of what happens when a parachute opens on a skydiver. The chute creates a lot of drag, slowing the parachuter down. On an airplane, there are several ways to increase the amount of drag. One is by extending flaps all the way down. But some airplanes use **speed brakes**, which are very strongly braced doors that extend from the fuselage or wings. Using speed brakes is a little like opening a barn door against the wind, but these devices can really help a jet fighter slow down in a hurry.

NASA F-15 with speed brake deployed behind cockpit.

Control Surface Variations

Most airplanes use conventional ailerons, rudders and elevators. But the only thing designers REALLY have to do is have SOME way of controlling the plane in all three dimensions of flight. Sometimes, the job a plane needs to do lends itself to a more unusual type of control design.

Photo courtesy of EAA

V-Tail Bonanza

On a conventional airplane tail, there are three surfaces that stick out from the airplane: the vertical tail (where the rudder is), and both sides of the horizontal (where the elevators are). Although most planes look like this, these three surfaces create a lot of drag because they stick out from the plane. (Remember – the nose of a smooth bullet is an ideal shape for low drag.)

The Beechcraft Bonanza is a single engine airplane designed for comfortable, fast cross-country travel. So its designers wanted to reduce its drag as much as possible while keeping it a comfortable, affordable travelling airplane. To help do this, they replaced the normal tail with a "V"-shaped tail. The V-tail only has two surfaces, and the V-angle of those surfaces helps reduce the drag even more. But how does this design allow rudder and elevator control?

Each side of the V has a moveable surface, sometimes called a **ruddervator**, which acts as both a **rudder** and an **elevator**. How? When both ruddervators are moved to the right or left, they act as a rudder (the curve creates lower pressure to one side, pushing the tail of the airplane left or right). When they are both moved inward or outward, they act as elevators. When they are both moved inward, for example, they increase the curve on the lower side of the V, pulling the tail of the plane down. The pilot doesn't have to think about this — he or she just moves the controls normally. The V-tail Bonanza isn't quite as stable as a conventional design (the tail **yaws**, or moves back and forth, more). But the V-tail does make the plane faster.

Close-up of Flying Wing controls

Photo courtesy of The Air Museum "Planes of Fame"

Flying Wing

Another weird airplane design is this Flying Wing. It was designed in the 1940s by the Northrop company in California. The idea was to make a plane that could carry a lot, fly a long distance, and still be fast. The flying wing was a good design for this because it had no tail to cause drag. (This is the last of these early Flying Wings. It still flies at an air museum in Chino, California.) Years later, the flying wing concept was used for the B-2 "Stealth Bomber," because a vertical tail is also easy to see on radar. If you take the vertical tail off an airplane, it becomes more "stealthy."

But if a plane has no tail at all, how do you control it? The Flying Wing has control surfaces, but they're all along the trailing edge of the wing. On each side of the cockpit, closest to the center, are normal flaps. Further out from that are **elevons**, which act as both **elevators** and **ailerons**. When the elevons go up and down together, they act as elevators. When one goes up and one goes down, they act as ailerons. At the wingtips, the wing has **split flaps** that act as both **rudders** and **speed brakes**. These little flaps split open, so the top half goes up and the bottom half goes down. When the pilot opens both wingtip split flaps at once, they act as speed brakes, creating drag on both sides and slowing the airplane down. If the split flap at just *one* wingtip is opened, it creates drag only on that side. That pulls that wingtip back, which works to turn the airplane left or right the same way as a rudder would.

The B-2 Stealth Bomber has the same kind of control system as this early flying wing, but the B-2 is easier to fly because its control movements are managed by a computer. So the plane feels more like a conventional airplane to the pilots who are flying it.

The Pathfinder and Centurion aircraft NASA is using for high-altitude research are also flying wing designs. Both planes use some of the same basic kind of controls as the Northrop Flying Wing. The Pathfinder and Centurion have **elevons**, but to make the plane turn, its controllers increase the power of the engines on one side of the plane while reducing the power on the other side's engines.

Canards

This unusual-looking airplane is called a Jetcruzer. Notice that its wing goes back to the tail of the airplane, almost like a delta wing. It doesn't have a horizontal tail at the back of the plane. Instead, the plane has a little wing at the front of the plane, called a **canard**. The plane's elevator is located on the canard, at the *front* of the plane instead of the back.

Why would a designer make a plane like this? Go back to the section on making airplanes stable. Remember how putting a horizontal tail on a plane helps balance it ? Try balancing a small model plane (or pencil) on top of one finger. Hard to do, isn't it? Now balance it on the tips of 2 fingers a little distance apart. Much easier, right? Well, adding a horizontal tail in addition to a wing does the same thing. But the way a horizontal stabilizer does this isn't necessarily the best way.

A typical wing, when it's creating lift, has a tendency to pitch the airplane *forward* (nose down). The horizontal tail balances this by actually creating **negative lift**, or by forcing the tail down. This keeps the nose of the airplane level. But it also takes away from the lift created by the wing. A **canard**, on the other hand, keeps the nose of the airplane from pitching down by creating **positive lift** at the nose of the airplane. Since both the wing and the canard are creating lift, a canard airplane is more efficient.

A canard also lets designers put an airplane wing further back while still keeping the plane balanced. In addition, many canard planes have no vertical tail. This can allow them to reduce the plane's drag. Instead of a vertical tail, the Jetcruzer has two vertical fins on the ends of its wing tips. These fins give the plane its directional stability and provide a place to put the plane's rudders.

The Jetcruzer's design makes it a comfortable business plane that can fly 360 mph on a single turboprop engine. (To learn more about turboprop engines, read the "Jet Engine" section.)

Photo courtesy of AASI Aircraft

NASA photo

Delta Wing Controls

Delta Wing planes (like the SST, the SR-71, or some European fighters) have one of the same problems as a Flying Wing — they have vertical tails, but they have no horizontal tail. So a delta wing design uses **elevons**, as well. Unlike the Flying Wing, delta wing designs generally don't have flaps, because their elevons take up most of the trailing edge of their wing. This is why they have their noses so high in the air when they land. Without flaps, the only way delta wing planes can fly slow enough to land is to have their wings at a very high **angle of attack**. Even then, delta wing designs still land at high speeds. So they need long runways.

AIRVENTURE!
The World's Biggest Fly-in, Oshkosh, Wisconsin

A supersonic transport is just one of thousands of amazing planes you can see at the EAA's annual fly-in! For a week each summer, the Wittman Airport in Oshkosh, Wisconsin turns into the busiest airport in the world. More than 12,000 airplanes and 750,000 people from around the world gather here for a week of activities, daily air shows, airplane camping, and fun in the sun. AirVenture's flight line includes everything from biplanes and taildraggers to ultralights, jets, and aerobatic wonders. Want an up-close look at any of the wings, engines, or flight controls discussed in this book? They're all at AirVenture!

KidVenture
As part of the AirVenture fly-in, a daily KidVenture program offers young people hands-on opportunities to learn more about flight and aircraft design. Participants get a chance to build and fly their own rockets and gliders, get tethered hot air balloon rides, practice with flight simulator programs, fly control line airplane models, and even meet aviation heroes like General Chuck Yeager and air show performer Patty Wagstaff.

For more information on AirVenture or KidVenture, contact the EAA at 920-426-4800 or look at the EAA's website at: www.eaa.org.

Photos courtesy of EAA

Cutting Edge Technology

Thrust Vectoring

As engineers have learned more about engines, materials, and design, they've been able to build wilder and more creative types of airplanes. They've also been able to design airplanes that could do things planes could never do before.

In the past few years, designers have been experimenting with a new way of making airplanes EXTREMELY maneuverable. All jet fighters until now have had very basic exhaust nozzles. The exhaust goes straight out the back. But designers have recently come up with ways of directing a jet engine's exhaust in different directions. This ability is called **thrust vectoring**, and it allows jets to make much sharper turns, change directions very quickly, and do maneuvers that used to be impossible.

NASA photo

How is a Jet Ski Like an Airplane?

How does thrust vectoring work? Just like a jet ski. A jet ski propels itself forward by funneling water out the back. To go straight, a jet ski keeps the exhaust water pointing straight behind the jet ski. If the water outlet at the back of the ski is turned so the water is shooting out toward the left side, the jet ski will turn to the left. If the water is turned, or "vectored" to the right, the jet ski turns to the right.

Thrust vectoring on a plane works the same way. If the jet exhaust is turned, or "vectored" right or left, it will turn the plane right or left. Because a plane also still has a rudder and ailerons, thrust vectoring adds an extra turning force that makes it turn and maneuver REALLY sharply. A plane can also "vector" its thrust up or down, letting the plane pitch up and down much faster, as well.

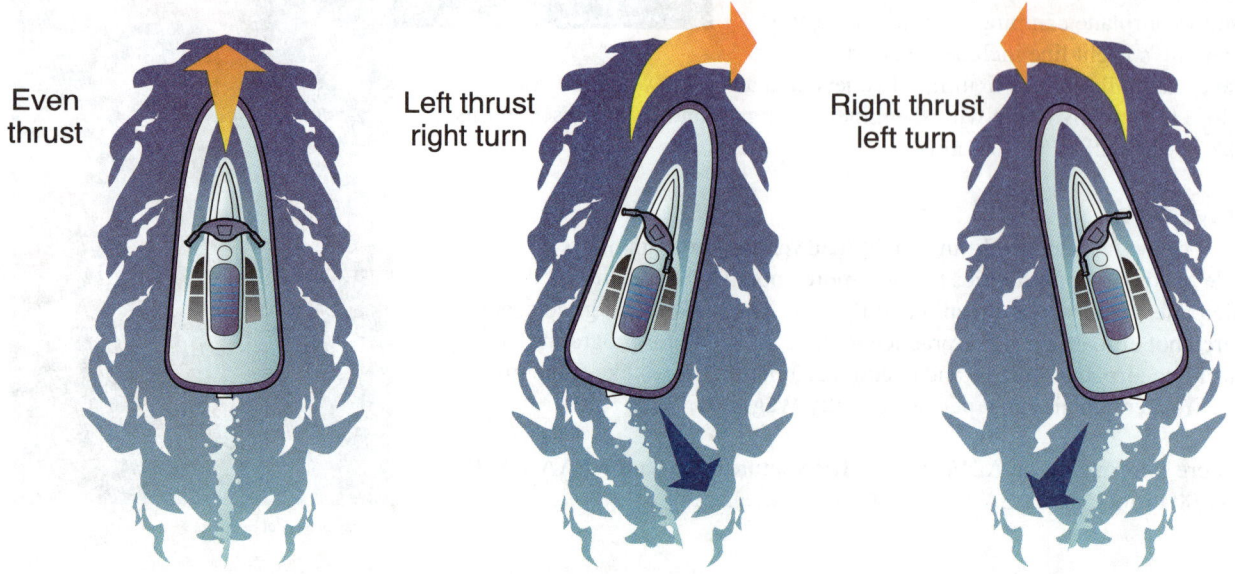

X-31

Another research plane that tested **thrust vectoring** was a delta wing jet called the X-31. It was a joint project between Germany and the United States to find out how thrust vectoring could improve a fighter plane's ability to maneuver and dogfight. Like the F-18 HARV, the X-31 used paddles behind its engine exhaust nozzles to change the direction (or "vector") of its exhaust.

How much of a difference did the thrust vectoring make? A lot. The X-31 was able to flip around and reverse its course quickly with its nose high in the air — which no other fighter could do. Because it was so maneuverable, the X-31 beat the other front-line fighters it was tested against 30 times for every time it lost!

NASA photo

F-18 HARV

One of the first airplanes to use thrust vectoring was this NASA F-18. It was a research plane flown at the Dryden Flight Research Center to learn more about how airplanes behave at VERY high angles of attack (or what test pilots call **high alpha**). The plane was called the F-18 "High Alpha Research Vehicle" (HARV). If researchers could get a plane to stay at high angles of attack, they could study how the air flow over the plane behaved at those angles. That would help engineers design better planes in the future. To make the plane able to do this, the researchers put moveable paddles behind the exhaust nozzles of the F-18 to direct its thrust left, right, up or down. This **thrust vectoring** kept the plane's nose up at a high angle and let the pilot control the plane even when its wings were at too steep an angle above the plane's flight path to create much lift or control.

NASA photo

AV-8 Harrier Jet

Long before the F-18 HARV or X-31 was flown, a plane called the "Harrier" was using thrust vectoring to do some amazing take-offs and landings. The exhaust from the Harrier's engines goes out through vents on the sides of the airplane, under its wings. The vents can be turned to direct the exhaust straight back, straight down, or any angle in between. If the vents are turned downward, the Harrier can take off almost like a helicopter, because its thrust is pushing straight down toward the ground. As the engine vents slowly move backward, they let the Harrier slowly pick up forward speed, until the exhaust is venting straight back and the plane is going forward at full speed. When the Harrier comes in to land, the vents can be slowly turned back toward the ground to slow the plane and let it touch down like a helicopter again. This lets the Harrier take off and land in places where there isn't enough space for a long runway.

X-36

Thrust vectoring can be used to make a fighter plane stable as well as to help it turn. So it might also be used to make a plane without a tail at all! Why would anyone want to design this kind of plane? Because a vertical tail is one of the most visible parts of an airplane on radar. If the tail could be eliminated, a plane would be much more "stealthy." The X-36 is a remote-controlled airplane that NASA researchers are using to test this "tailless airplane" idea.

F-15 ACTIVE

Taking thrust vectoring one step further, NASA tested a plane called the F-15 Advanced Controls Technology for Integrated Vehicles (ACTIVE). Instead of using paddles to deflect its exhaust, the F-15 ACTIVE's exhaust nozzles actually swiveled around to aim the exhaust in different directions. This was an important step, because paddles are too heavy to be used on real fighter planes. In order for future fighters to have thrust vectoring, engine companies probably will have to develop some kind of swiveling or moveable exhaust nozzles.

Real Life Profile: Jamail Larkins
15 years old, Young Eagle, Student Pilot, Augusta, GA

Jamail Larkins was always interested in planes, but he didn't know how to get involved in flying. Then he heard about the Young Eagles program. The Young Eagles program is sponsored by the Experimental Aircraft Association and matches young people who want airplane rides with pilots who are willing to give them those rides.

After one flight as a Young Eagle, Larkins was hooked. He started volunteering with the program, and on Larkins' 13th birthday, the local Young Eagles coordinator gave him his first official flight lesson. Since then, Larkins has earned money for additional lessons by selling flight materials over the Internet. He's also gotten flying time with pilots he's met through the Young Eagles and by just hanging around the airport.

"I always thought I MIGHT be interested in flying," he says. "That first flight with the Young Eagles made me SURE."

Space Controls

What if you had to control a plane or vehicle in space? What would be the biggest problem you'd face? Think about it. Control surfaces, whether they're on a wing, a tail, or a canard, rely on air passing over them to work. But in space there's no air. That means control surfaces won't work. So how does a spacecraft steer?

Answer: The same way a thrust-vectoring airplane does. In space, the only way to turn or control a spacecraft is by using **thrust**. Almost all spacecraft have small rocket motors, called **reaction controls**, that can be fired to turn or control the vehicle.

NASA photo

X-15

The first plane to really use reaction controls was the X-15. (See "Fast Wings" for more on the X-15.) Although it didn't go into orbit, the X-15 flew high enough that at points in the flight it didn't have enough air molecules going over it for its control surfaces to work. At the edge of space, the pilot controlled the X-15 with small **reaction controls** on its nose and on the tips of its wings. Firing different reaction controls made the X-15 pitch up or down and roll left or right.

NASA photo

Space Shuttle

The Space Shuttle also uses reaction controls to control its movement in space. It has 44 different reaction control rockets that it fires to keep it on course. Usually, the Shuttle's computers control the firing of the rockets. But when the Shuttle picks up a satellite or docks with another spacecraft, the pilots steer the Shuttle by operating these reaction controls themselves. The controls are so precise that the Shuttle pilots can position the Shuttle with less than 6 inches of error!

Real Life Profile: Curt Brown
NASA Space Shuttle Commander, Pilot, Houston, Texas

Curt Brown started taking flying lessons when he was in high school with money he earned repairing television sets. But he didn't think he'd ever become an astronaut. Still, Brown went to college and then became an Air Force pilot. And when he then applied to be an astronaut, NASA picked him. "It taught me that if there's something you want to do, you need to just go after it and not let anyone tell you you can't," he says.

What's the most amazing thing about going into space? "We think we know so much," he says. "But you get out there in the blackness of space and stars, and you realize how much there is that we know nothing about."

When he's not in space, Brown also loves air racing and flying his Christen Eagle aerobatic biplane. "Flying government planes, you always have a certain job to do," he explains. "Flying the biplane, I have total freedom to fly how I want."

NASA's "Flying Bedsteads"

One of the most ambitious control feats ever attempted in space was the first landing on the moon in 1969. The Lunar Module, which separated from a command module and descended from an orbit around the Moon to the Moon's surface, had no wings or lifting surfaces at all. Wings or control surfaces wouldn't have done any good, because the vehicle was only going to fly in space, where there isn't any air. The Lunar Module was a boxy-shaped spacecraft, and the only way the astronauts could slow it down, turn it, or control it was by using thrust from numerous reaction controls around the spacecraft.

Designers wanted a way to make sure the lunar lander would work and a way to teach the astronauts how to fly the lander, in case the astronauts had to take over from the computerized autopilot. After all, the astronauts would have only one chance at a landing. If something went wrong, they might not ever get back home. This weird-looking aircraft was Dryden's solution to NASA's problem. It was called the LLRV — which stood for the Lunar Lander Research Vehicle. The LLRV looked so much like an old iron bedframe that it got the nickname "The Flying Bedstead." But even though it looked strange, it successfully imitated the behavior of the lunar lander on the moon.

How did it do that? First, the LLRV had a jet engine in the middle of it that put out just enough thrust to support 5/6 of its weight. Can you guess why the designers wanted to do that? It's because the Moon only has one-sixth the gravity of Earth. So the jet engine made the LLRV weigh the same amount here as the lunar lander would weigh on the moon. The astronaut flying the LLRV then used **reaction controls** to tilt the LLRV in one direction or another.

In test flights, the astronauts would take the LLRV up a few hundred feet and then practice maneuvering it down to a landing, using the reaction controls. If that sounds hard, it's because it *was* hard. But the training paid off. When Neil Armstrong was taking the real lunar lander down to the Moon's surface for the first time, he realized the landing spot the computer autopilot was steering them toward wasn't smooth enough for a safe landing. So he took over and was able to land the lunar module somewhere else, thanks to the training he got in NASA's Flying Bedsteads here on Earth.

NASA photo

NASA photo

Satellites

Even spacecraft without pilots use reaction controls to move around and maintain their orbits. Almost every satellite in orbit today (and there are lots of them!) carries a fuel supply on board to power small reaction controls that stabilize it, change the satellite's position or boost it to a higher orbit. Some of these satellites are really HUGE. One telescope that's in orbit now weighs more than 34,000 pounds. That's as much weight as 17 cars piled on top of one another! But since there's almost no gravity in space, something that weighs 34,000 pounds here is light as a feather up there.

Real Life Profile: Kathy Thornton
NASA Astronaut, Ph.D. Physicist, Charlottesville, VA

Kathy Thornton still remembers the day she saw the ad for astronaut positions at NASA and realized it didn't take a superwoman to become an astronaut. "They were just looking for healthy people with a technical, math and science background," she says.

Thornton, who has a Ph.D. degree in physics, was accepted into the program and went into space as a mission specialist on the Space Shuttle four times. She helped repair an Intelsat satellite on one exciting mission and helped service the Hubble Space Telescope on another.

"Being an astronaut was great," she says, "because every day was different. I was always learning something new." But the best part was getting the chance to try life without gravity. "You can bring back pictures from space, but you can't bring back that sensation of floating," she says. "That's what I miss about space the most."

Engines

Another critical part of any aircraft design is what kind of engine the plane has in it. After all, without an engine, few airplanes will go very far. But just as different types of wings let airplanes do different types of things, the kind of engine a plane has will also determine what it can do well.

There are four basic types of engines used in aircraft and spacecraft.

Piston

Piston engines are probably the most common type of engine. Cars, motorcycles, and even lawn mowers run on piston engines. So do many kinds of airplanes. Piston engines are relatively simple to build, which means they don't cost that much, and they don't burn a lot of fuel. On the other hand, piston engines are more limited in the amount of thrust they can produce than jet engines, and they work much better at low altitudes than at high altitudes. So piston engines are good for simple airplanes, airplanes that don't need to fly fast, or airplanes that fly at lower altitudes (lower than the altitudes where airliners fly).

Photo courtesy of EAA

Turbojet

Turbojet, or "jet" engines were developed during World War II. They create a lot of thrust, and they work well even at high altitudes where the air is really thin. But they are more expensive to build and operate than a piston engine. So jet engines work best for airplanes that need to fly high and fast, or need a lot of power for some other reason.

Some jet engines have propellers connected to them. Airplanes with these engines are called **turboprops**, because they are a mix between a turbojet and a propeller-driven airplane. A turboprop offers some of the efficiency of a piston engine with more speed and reliability than a typical piston engine. But the propeller makes a turboprop slower than a pure jet airplane.

Photo courtesy of Raytheon Aircraft and Paul Bowen

Ramjet

Ramjet and Scramjet Engines don't have any moving parts at all. As its name implies, a ramjet "rams" air through an engine tube, ignites it and sends the exhaust out the back. But a ramjet only works at extremely high speeds. A Scramjet is short for "Supersonic Ramjet," and it only works at supersonic speeds. So these engines are only good for planes that go REALLY fast. At the moment, there are no operational airplanes that use a ramjet or a scramjet. But NASA is testing these designs because they might be used in the future for a high-speed supersonic airliner or even hypersonic plane. (A hypersonic plane is one that flies five or more times faster than sound travels.)

NASA's Hyper X

Rocket

Rocket Engines create a tremendous explosive force and don't need air to mix with their fuel in order for it to burn. This is why we've used rocket engines to test our fastest research airplanes (such as the X-1 and the X-15) and to get spacecraft into space, where there is no air. The disadvantage of rocket engines is that since they have to carry both fuel and a substitute for air, called an "oxidizer," to make the fuel burn, instead of mixing their own fuel supply with outside air, they can't run for very long. So they're good for getting cargo into space, but they'd be bad for powering an airliner.

Rocket engines typically mix hydrogen or some other explosive chemical with liquid oxygen (which they use instead of outside air to make the fuel burn). Most piston and jet engines burn fuel and air. But there are a few airplanes that run on electric power or some other kind of alternative fuel. One designer even got an airplane engine to work with bicycle power! Keep reading to find out more about how these machines work.

Real Life Profile: Marta Bohn-Meyer
Research Engineer, SR-71 Flight Engineer
NASA Dryden Flight Research Center, Edwards, CA

Marta Bohn-Meyer is the fastest-flying woman alive. She is the only woman SR-71 crew member in the world. Bohn-Meyer is also an aerobatic pilot, but it was her degree in aeronautical engineering that got her a seat in the Mach 3 Blackbird.

"You can't be a good flight test engineer without being a good ground engineer," she says. "Even our best test pilots are researchers at heart."

The great thing about working at Dryden Flight Research Center, according to Bohn-Meyer, is that "what you can do is only limited by your own imagination." But flying in the Blackbird is unquestionably the highlight of Bohn-Meyer's job. "It's physically and technically challenging to fly in that plane," she says. "So it's very satisfying to do it well...especially when you realize that you're doing something that only 470 or so people have ever done."

Piston Engines

Piston engines are the most common type of airplane engine. They're used in almost all small airplanes, because they're less expensive to build, run, and maintain than jets are. They also work much better at slow speeds and low to the ground, which is where most small airplanes fly.

Bicycle Pumps and Piston Engines

How does a piston engine work? A little like a bicycle pump, actually. Think about how a bike pump works. You first pull the handle up, drawing air into the cylinder of the pump. You then push the handle down, which pushes a plate, or piston, inside the cylinder down on top of that air, forcing the air out the bottom and into your bike tire. You then pull the handle up again and repeat the motion.

Now what would happen if you didn't have a hole at the bottom of the pump for the air to escape into your tire? When you pushed the pump handle down, you would be *compressing* the air, squishing the molecules very close together and putting the air under a lot of pressure. Now say you had some fuel mist mixed in with the air in the cylinder when you pushed the handle down. And when you got the handle all the way down, so the air was compressed at the bottom, you lit a match to that high-pressure air and fuel. What do you think would happen?

KA-BOOM! That's what would happen. And that explosion would drive the handle and piston back up to the top of the cylinder with a whole lot of force. Now say you decided the explosion was so neat that you wanted to try it again. The cylinder would be filled with the smoke and exhaust from the first explosion. So you'd first have to push the handle (and piston) down to clear the cylinder of the polluted air (assuming you had an exhaust hole at the bottom of the cylinder). Then you'd bring the handle back up to fill the cylinder with fresh air and push the handle down to compress that air. Then you could light a spark or match to it and watch it explode again.

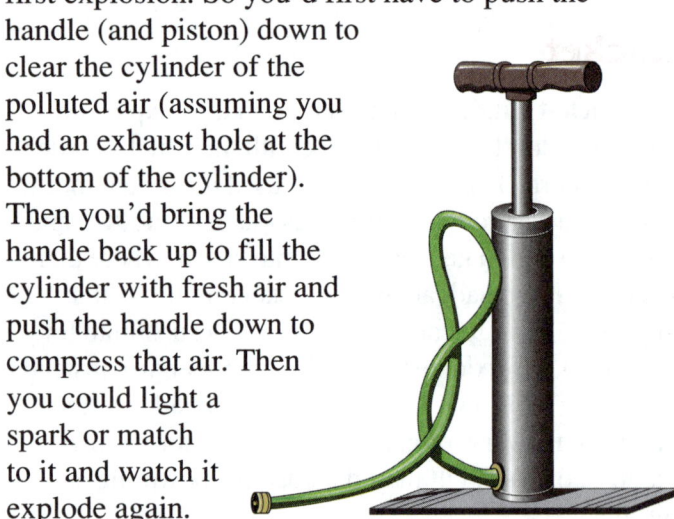

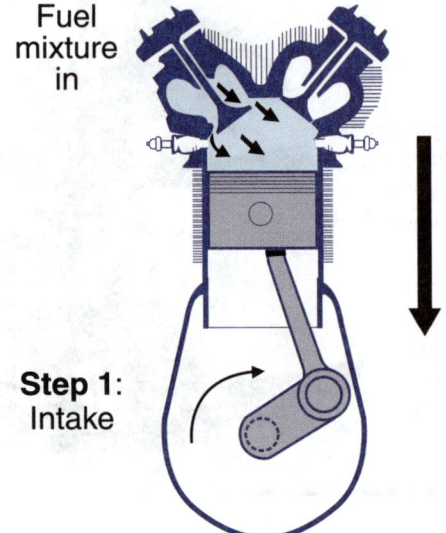

Step 1: Intake

Fuel mixture in

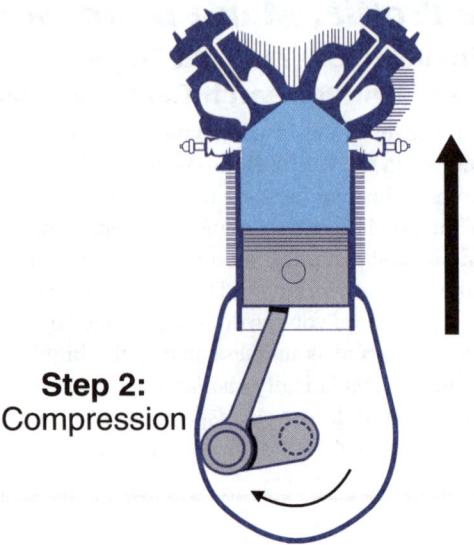

Step 2: Compression

Photo courtesy of Textron-Lycoming

This is how most piston engines work. Whether it's in your car or in your airplane, piston engines are made up of **cylinders**, connected to something called a **crankshaft**. Within each cylinder is a piston that moves up and down in four steps:

1. The piston moves up, letting air and fuel into the cylinder.

2. The piston moves down, compressing that air and fuel.

3. A spark lights off that compressed air and fuel, causing an explosion and slamming the piston back up to the top of the cylinder.

4. The piston moves back down again, clearing the cylinder of the exhaust gases.

Then the cycle starts all over again. This happens in every cylinder of your engine, thousands of times every minute. But how do these movements drive the propeller of an airplane? Because all the pistons are connected to a turning rod called a **crankshaft**.

As the pistons move up and down, they hit bumps on the crankshaft, making it spin around. A crankshaft is like the pedals of your bike. If you had pistons moving up and down under the pedals of your bike, it would force your feet up – first right, then left, then right again. That would make the pedals turn. In a plane, the crankshaft is connected to the propeller. So the faster the pistons turn the crankshaft, the faster the propeller turns.

All these piston and crankshaft movements happen EXTREMELY fast. If people say an engine is turning 3,000 "RPM," they mean that the crankshaft is rotating 3,000 times per minute. "RPM" stands for "Revolutions (or turns) Per Minute. That's a lot! Try spinning around while standing in your living room and see how many times you can spin in a minute. It's a lot less than three thousand!

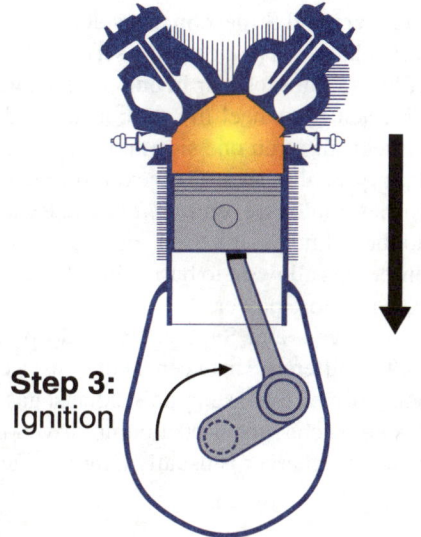

Step 3: Ignition

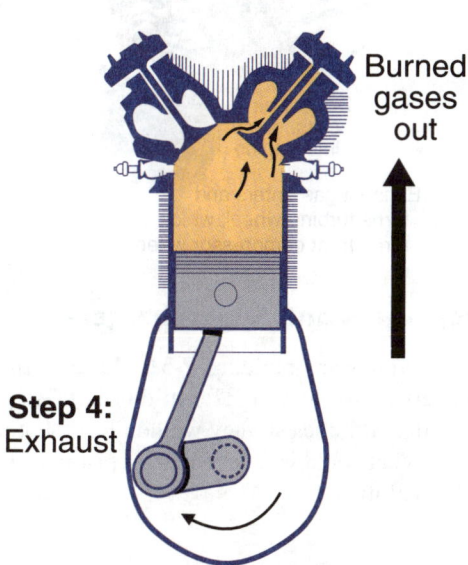

Burned gases out

Step 4: Exhaust

Types of Piston Engines

There are several types of piston engines. Some of the very earliest airplane engines didn't have a way to make the crankshaft and propeller turn separately from the engine. So the cylinders were arranged in a circle around the crankshaft, and the WHOLE ENGINE spun around with the propeller! These spinning engines were called **rotary radial engines**.

Designers moved on from these clunky spinning engines pretty quickly, but many early planes used radial engines. One of the advantages of a radial engine was that the front side of all the cylinders was exposed to the air. This was important because every piston engine has to have a way of cooling. Most piston airplane engines are *air-cooled*, meaning they rely on air flowing over baffles, or radiator-type fins on the outside of the cylinders, to cool them down.

Another type of piston engine is a *water-cooled* engine. Most cars except Volkswagon Beetles use water-cooled piston engines. The radiator at the front of the car holds a fluid. Fresh air passes over the radiator and cools the fluid, and the cooled fluid runs around the engine, cooling the cylinders. Some airplane engines have been designed to be water cooled

One way to get more power for an airplane is to put on an engine with more cylinders, or bigger cylinders. But another option is to simply add a second or third or fourth engine. Multi-engine airplanes also have the advantage that if one engine quits, the airplane will still have one or more engines creating power to fly.

(the P-51 Mustangs in WWII used water-cooled engines). A water-cooled engine lets you have a sleeker engine, since you don't need to expose all the cylinders to the air. But it adds weight, since you need to carry water to cool the cylinders.

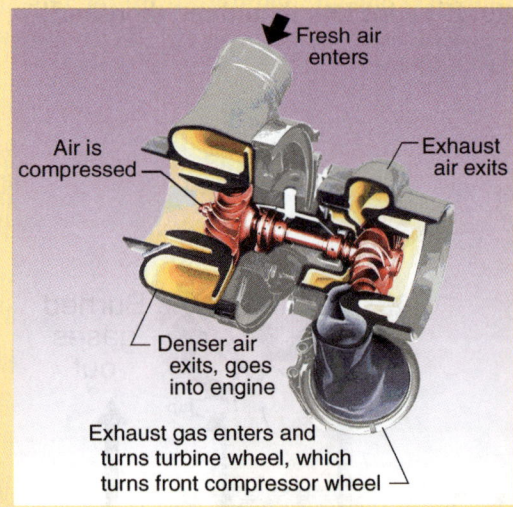

Turbochargers and Superchargers

What if you were building P-51 Mustang fighters or B-17 bombers in World War II? You'd need these planes to fly at very high altitudes so they wouldn't get shot down by ground fire. What could you do to make a piston engine work better at high altitude?

The problem is that there aren't very many air molecules at high altitudes. And since air and fuel only burn in a specific mixture, less dense air burns a smaller amount of fuel. So it produces less power.

To get more power, you need to make the air more dense in order to allow more fuel to burn with it. How do you do that? By squishing, or compressing, lots of air together into a smaller area before adding fuel or a spark to it. This is what **Turbochargers** and **Superchargers** do.

A turbocharger is made up of a series of fan-like wheels. Think of how a fan sucks air in on one side and blows it out the other. Each fan wheel in a turbocharger does the same thing. It sucks air in on one side and pushes it out the other into a slightly smaller area. The next fan wheel sucks that air in and pushes it into an even *smaller* area. By the time the air goes into the cylinders, it's been squished a lot, so it's much more dense. This allows it to burn with a lot more fuel, which produces a lot more power.

Turbochargers and Superchargers do pretty much the same job. The difference between them is that a **turbocharger** uses a pump driven by the engine's exhaust gas to turn its fan wheels. A **supercharger** uses a pump driven by the engine itself. So a turbocharger is usually a more efficient design.

Photo courtesy of EAA

Fast Piston Engines

What if you wanted to make a airplane with a piston engine go REALLY fast? What would you do? You'd do what these guys do. They race highly modified WWII fighters every year at the Reno, Nevada National Championship Air Races. The only rule is that the planes have to have piston engines and propellers (in other words, no jets allowed). The race teams usually use WWII fighter planes because these planes were the fastest propeller planes we ever made before we started making jets. The racers then soup up the engines of these planes something fierce.

First, they use turbochargers or superchargers to make the air dense before it goes into the engine. Since cooler air is more dense than hot air (re-read the first section on "The Atmosphere" if you forget how this works), some planes also use nitrous oxide gas to super-cool the air going into the engine. This makes the air really dense, so it can mix with more fuel and make more power. Many racers then put an alcohol-water mixture into the cylinders along with the fuel to cool the fuel-air mixture and keep it from overheating and exploding too soon. What else? Many racers have sprinkler systems that spray water on either the cylinders (in an air-cooled engine) or on the front of the radiator (in a water-cooled engine). This helps the plane go faster because, once again, cooler air is more dense and creates more power.

In addition to increasing the thrust of race planes, racers also try to reduce drag as much as possible. Racers will make the wings shorter, streamline the cockpit canopy, make the wings smoother, and add special wingtips and coverings to reduce the amount of drag the airplane produces.

The result? Some of these planes fly around this oval race course, 50 feet off the ground, at almost 500 miles an hour. That means they fly more than two football field lengths every second!

Real Life Profile: Adam McCartney
18 years old, *Dreadnought* Racing Team Jackson, CA

The planes Adam McCartney works on are more than three times older than he is. But that's part of the appeal. A few years ago, McCartney's cousin was working for a company that restores – and races – World War II fighter airplanes. McCartney tagged along with his cousin to work one day. Soon he was working at Sanders Aircraft any time he wasn't in school. He also crewed for the shop's "Dreadnought" Unlimited air racing team at the Reno National Air Races.

"I feel real lucky," he says. "The first year I went to Reno, my jaw was on the ground the whole time. I've met all these interesting people, and this has really taught me that hard work always gets results."

McCartney's learned a lot about working on airplanes. But the best part is that his job gets him the chance to fly. "There's nothing quite like loading Gs," he says. "And when you're up there, you're not thinking about yesterday or tomorrow. You're just thinking about where you are right now, and that's great."

Jet Engines

There are lots of ways to make a piston engine airplane go faster, or fly higher. But if you really want an airplane to go fast, nothing beats a jet. Of course, a jet is not a very efficient kind of engine. It burns a lot more fuel than a piston engine will (at least until it reaches high altitudes). But a jet engine keeps producing power up high, where pistons don't work as well. And it can make an airplane fly at very high speeds.

NASA photo

How Does a Jet Engine Work?

Jets work pretty much the same way that turbochargers and superchargers do. In a jet engine, a series of fan-like wheels, one behind another, each sucks air through it and pushes the air into a smaller space behind it. The section of the engine with these fan-like wheels is called the "compressor" section, because the wheels squeeze, or compress, the air. As the air is compressed, it gets more dense (and capable of producing more power). The compressed air then passes into a combustion chamber. In the combustion chamber, fuel is mixed with air and then ignited, shooting the exhaust air out the back of the engine. This is what creates a jet engine's thrust. When a jet engine is started, igniters light a small amount of fuel in the combustion chamber. After that, fuel and air are always flowing into the chamber. So a jet engine is constantly burning fuel and creating thrust out the back of the engine.

On its way out of the engine, the jet's exhaust air turns another series of fan-like wheels, called "turbines." These "turbine" wheels are connected by a long shaft to the compressor blades (the fan-type wheels) at the front of the engine. So the exhaust air turns the back turbine blades, which, in turn, make the front "compressor" blades turn, which compresses more air into the engine, creating more power and causing more air to shoot out the back, which turns the turbine blade sections, which then turns the front compressor blade sections, and so on, in a cycle.

The official name of a jet engine is actually a **turbine** engine, named after the whirling fan-like sections of blades that operate the engine. The word turbine means "whirlwind." This is also where the name **turbocharger** comes from ("turbine charger").

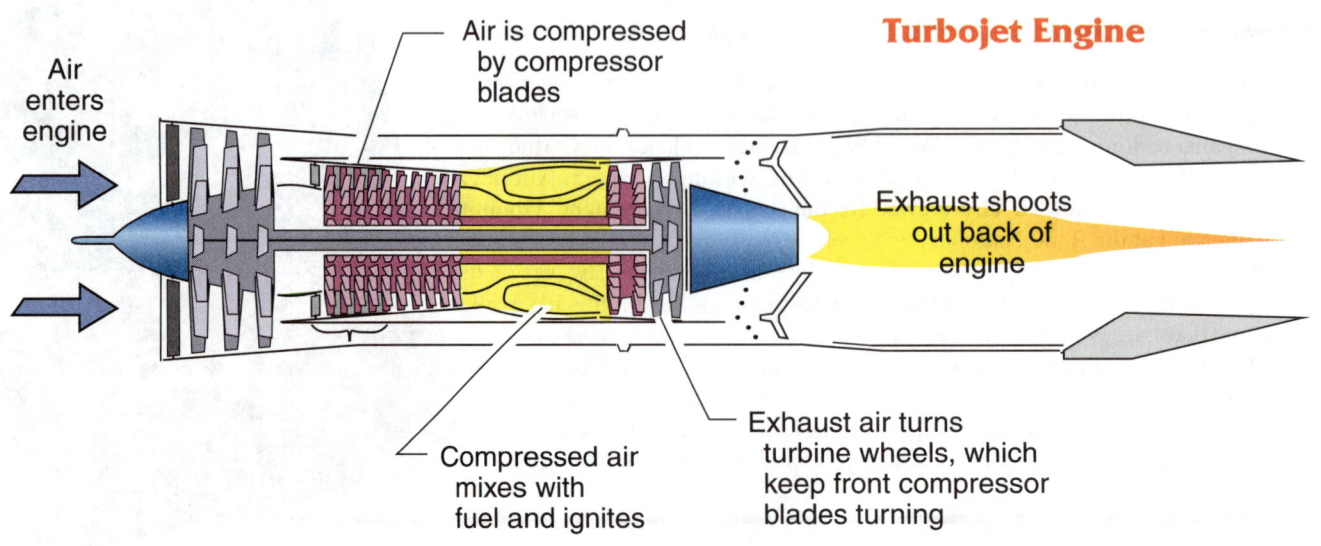

Turbojet Engine

Turbine Power

Turbofan Engine

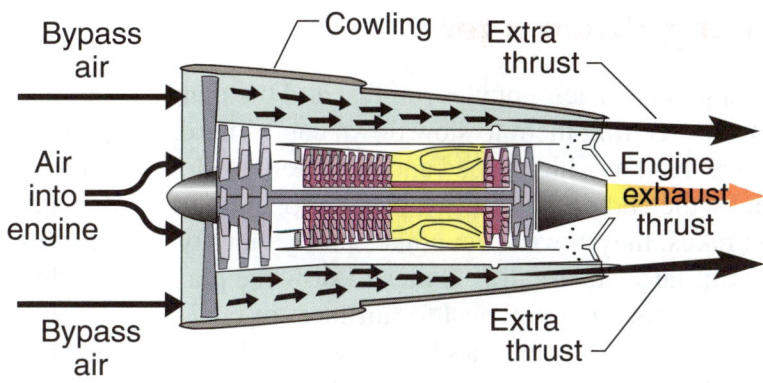

Just like there are different kinds of piston engines, there are different kinds of jet engines. The most straightforward kind of jet engine is a turbojet engine. All the air going into the front of the engine **inlet** (opening) of a **turbojet** is compressed and sent through the engine, and all of the engine's thrust comes from its exhaust coming out the back.

A **turboprop** engine operates a lot like a turbojet, except the power from the engine is used to turn a propeller. The exhaust gas turns turbine wheels that are connected to a shaft. That shaft is connected to the propeller at the front of the engine. So the thrust in a turboprop engine is created by the propeller, not by the simple exhaust gas going out the back of the engine.

Why would someone want to use this kind of engine? Because it's more efficient than a straight turbojet. Since its thrust comes from a propeller, a turboprop doesn't have to make as much power to create the same amount of thrust as a straight turbojet. But the propeller limits the speed of a turbojet. Propellers can only turn so fast before their tips start breaking the speed of sound. Since each propeller blade is really a little wing, supersonic speed creates shock waves on the propeller blades, which make them stop working well. So a turboprop works well on business planes or commuter planes that fly at higher altitudes but don't have to fly as fast as an airliner or a fighter jet.

A **turbofan** engine is simply a more efficient kind of **turbojet**. Most airliner engines today are turbofan engines. In a turbofan, not all of the air going into the engine inlet goes into the engine. A big fan at the front of the engine sends all the incoming air back into the engine compartment. But some of the air in a turbofan engine goes AROUND the engine and straight out the back. It's almost as if you took a turbojet engine and put it inside a bigger engine compartment. You still get the same thrust out of the engine as a normal turbojet. But you ALSO get some "free" thrust from the air being shoved backward from the big fan in front. Since it doesn't go through the engine, it doesn't burn any fuel. It just adds some extra thrust. But if you just wanted speed, and didn't care how much fuel you burned, you might not choose a turbofan, because a turbofan has a bigger opening at the front. This creates more drag than a turbojet engine opening. So like everything else in airplane design, what kind of jet engine you choose depends on what you want the airplane to do.

NASA photo

Beech King Air Turboprop

Slowing Down a Jet

Jets go fast. Their engines run fast and the planes fly fast. So getting them to slow down can be hard. Most jets land at a high speed and need help to slow down by the end of the runway. If the pilots just used brakes, they'd wear out brakes pretty quickly. Some military jets use drag chutes to slow the plane down. But that's not practical for airliners or business jets. So most jet engines have a way of deflecting the thrust from the engine *forward*, which, if you remember Newton's law, causes the airplane to move *backward*. Since the jet is moving forward so quickly, the plane doesn't really move backward. It just slows down. These devices are called **thrust reversers**, and they're usually sturdy pieces of metal that can be extended or moved behind the engine's exhaust to force it forward. If you've ever been on an airliner, you might have noticed that the engine noise gets a lot louder right after it lands. This is the sound of its thrust reversers turning the air forward.

Turboprop engines also have the ability to reverse their thrust, but they use the propeller to do it. They can switch the angle of the propeller blades so that it's like turning a bedroom fan around. When a turboprop engine switches the angle of its propeller blades, the propeller blows air *forward* instead of *backward*. This does the same thing as a jet sending its exhaust thrust forward instead of backward.

Turboprops can do one other thing, as well. Say you're flying the turboprop engine-powered Pilatus PC-6 Porter pictured here, which is good for jobs like carrying skydivers and other cargo, and landing on very short runways. Your skydivers have just jumped overboard, and there are more waiting on the runway right beneath you. You want to get down as quickly as possible. You can put the propeller blades in a totally flat angle, so the blades become a flat disc at the front of the plane. The propeller becomes a big, draggy speed brake on the front of the plane. Now the pilot can point the nose almost straight down toward the runway and lose a whole lot of altitude really quickly without gaining too much speed. It's a pretty exciting way to approach a runway, but it's very useful if you need to get down quickly.

Photo courtesy of Pilatus Aircraft and Thomas Hunziker

Pilatus PC-6 Porter

How a Jet Thrust-Reverser Works

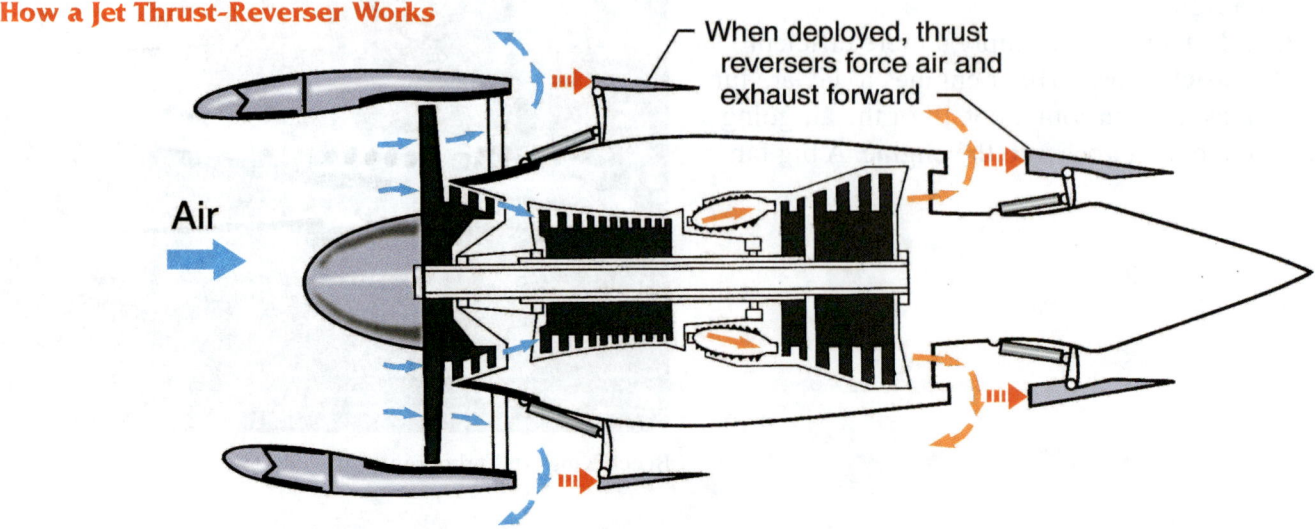

When deployed, thrust reversers force air and exhaust forward

Air

98

NASA photo

Afterburners

Afterburners are one of those cool, fighter plane tricks that let a plane tear a hole in the sky and leave every other plane in the dust of its wake. Afterburners do this by giving a plane an extra kick of thrust. How? An afterburner feeds extra fuel into the exhaust gas coming out of the engine. This fuel ignites, creating more thrust. But afterburners use a lot of fuel, so you don't want to use them all the time or you'll run out of fuel VERY quickly.

Real Life Profile: Heather Penny
24 years old, Air National Guard Fighter Pilot
Witchita Falls, TX

For a while, Heather Penny couldn't decide which she wanted to do more: study literature or fly fighter jets. The jets won.

Penny earned her private pilot's license during her freshman year of college, but didn't have much money to fly after that. So she concentrated on her other studies, earning a degree in literature. But she finally decided she wanted to fly F-16s. So she started applying to Air National Guard units.

Last year, the Washington, D.C. guard unit offered her a job. "I'm going to work full-time for the guard as long as I can," she says. When her guard work becomes part-time, she thinks she might like to try her hand at "firebombing" — fighting forest fires from an airplane. That is, if she doesn't teach literature.

"I've figured out that the thing to do is find something to do that doesn't feel like work," she says, "and the rest will come. That's what flying is for me. I can't believe they're paying me to do this."

Alternate Fuel Engines

Most aircraft engines are either pistons or jets. And most of them run on aviation gas (which is a lot like car gas), or jet fuel (which is very much like the kerosene you might use in a heater or camping lantern). But there are some aircraft engines that run on very different types of fuel systems.

Gossamer Albatross

In 1959, a prize for 50,000 British pounds (about $100,000 in U.S. dollars today) was offered for the first person to achieve sustained, controlled, *human-powered* flight. The prize was won in 1977 by a designer named Paul MacCready, who designed the *Gossamer Condor* airplane. The plane was powered by its pilot turning pedals with his feet. The pedals were connected through gears to a propeller on a long shaft. So when he turned the pedals, the pilot was turning the propeller.

In order for a single person to create enough power to lift the plane off the ground, the plane had to be very light. So the Gossamer Condor's wings and bare-bones fuselage were covered in a lightweight plastic covering. The entire covering on the airplane weighed only 2 pounds!

Two years later, MacCready built a bigger version of the plane called the *Albatross* (pictured below). The Albatross, which was also powered by a person pedalling its propeller, was the first human-powered airplane to cross the English Channel.

NASA photo

Perseus

NASA photo

This Perseus airplane uses another kind of alternative-fuel engine. The Perseus was designed for slow, long-endurance, high-altitude flight, just like the Pathfinder. Why do both of these high-altitude planes use alternative-fuel engines? Because their designers had to solve the same basic problem: piston engines don't work well at high altitudes. At extremely high altitudes, the air is much less dense than it is at sea level, so there aren't enough air molecules to mix with fuel to get enough power to make the plane fly.

A jet can work in thin air, but a jet uses a lot of fuel, especially while it's *getting* up to high altitude. A plane that uses a lot of fuel either can't stay up very long or has to carry a lot of fuel. But if it carries a lot of fuel, it will be very heavy, which will keep it from getting up to a very high altitude without even more power, which will take more fuel ... etc.

To get these airplanes to stay up a long time at very high altitudes, the planes needed very efficient, lightweight engines. The Pathfinder and Centurion used solar-powered electric motors, so they didn't have to carry any fuel. The Perseus used a lightweight piston engine, instead. To solve the problem of having to use high-altitude air, which would be too thin to mix with much fuel, the Perseus used a unique "closed" air system. Instead of dumping exhaust air overboard, the Perseus engine recycled the air, mixing it with liquid oxygen before putting it back into the engine. Liquid oxygen is very dense, so the air/liquid oxygen mixture acted and burned like low-altitude air.

The Pathfinder/Centurion

The same man who designed the pedal-powered Condor and Albatross went on to design the two long-range, high-altitude gossamer-wing airplanes tested by NASA. The Pathfinder (with a 120-foot long wing) and the bigger Centurion (with a 206-foot long wing) are both solar powered airplanes. Solar collecting cells on the top of the plane convert energy from the sun to electric power. That power runs the electric motors that turn the propellers. There are no pistons or compressors in an electric motor. Just like a little radio-controlled airplane model, the electric power simply turns gears, which turn the crankshaft and propeller.

NASA photo

Supersonic Engines

Supersonic jet fighters may fly faster than the speed of sound, but the air going into their engines is slowed down below the speed of sound before it hits their turbine blades. Designers have to make the engines do this because supersonic air creates shock waves. In a jet engine, those shock waves would keep the air from flowing smoothly through the moving turbine wheels.

But a plane flying faster than Mach 3 or more (2,200 - 4,000 miles per hour) can't slow the air down that much. So it needs a different kind of engine.

Ramjets

A ramjet is a kind of jet engine. But it has no moving parts. The air is compressed just by being "rammed" into the opening of the engine. As it passes through this tube-like engine, the compressed air is then mixed with fuel and lit. Then, just like a jet, the exhaust is sent out the back, creating thrust. But in order for the air to be compressed simply by the airplane's speed, the airplane has to be travelling very fast. So ramjets only work at speeds higher than 300 miles an hour — faster than the fastest drag car! And they only get really effective at speeds above the speed of sound (about 750 miles per hour). So one of the problems with a ramjet is how to get the plane up to a speed where the ramjet will work.

Right now, there are no airplanes that use a ramjet. But engineers are thinking about using a ramjet for an airliner of the future that could go 2 or 3 times the speed of sound.

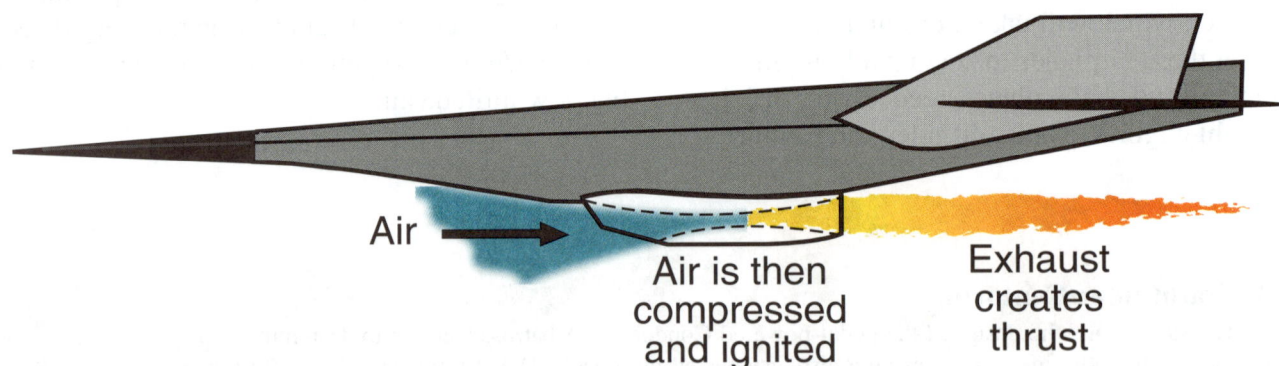

Air → Air is then compressed and ignited — Exhaust creates thrust

Scramjets

A scramjet is really a "Supersonic Combustion RAMJET." It's still an air-breathing engine, like a jet, and it works very much like a ramjet. The difference is that the speed of the air going through a scramjet is always faster than the speed of sound. So a scramjet would only work for a plane designed to go VERY fast. NASA is building a model plane called the Hyper X to test a scramjet engine. To give you an idea of how fast a scramjet engine can go, the Hyper X model is being built to fly between Mach 7 and Mach 10. That's 7 or 10 times faster than sound travels, or as fast as 7,000 miles an hour!

Extra Credit: The SR-71's Weird Engines

The SR-71 is the fastest airplane in the world. It flies faster than Mach 3 (about 2,200 miles per hour) and flies over 80,000 feet, or 16 miles above the ground! Its engines are not rockets. They are air-breathing jet engines. But they are very unusual jet engines.

When the SR-71 is travelling at Mach 3 or faster, the pointy spikes that stick out from the front of its engine inlets move partway back into the engine inlets. This lets the shock wave from the supersonic air coming into the engine move *inside* the inlet.

Now imagine you're an air molecule flowing through the SR-71's engine. You'd enter the inlet, flow into the combustion chamber, get mixed with fuel and get shot out the exhaust nozzles in the back. But a shock wave disturbs and slows down air as the air flows past it. So as an air molecule, you'd be moving faster when you first entered the engine inlet. As you passed through the shock wave, you'd slow down.

Now think back to what you know about lift. Faster moving air has lower pressure than slower moving air, right? (Remember the garden hose and why wings create lift.) So you and your buddy air molecules would have a *lower pressure* when you first entered the engine inlet (when you were moving faster) than after you passed through the shock wave and slowed down. And if you remember, air and objects want to move *toward* areas of low pressure air (this is why curve balls curve and wings fly). So the slower, higher-pressure air that has already passed through the shock wave — and which is now further toward the *back* of the plane — actually wants to move *forward*.

This desire of the high-pressure air to move toward the *front* of the inlet, where the air pressure is lower, is so great that it actually draws the SR-71 forward through the air! By the time the SR-71 is flying Mach 3, as much as 60% of the plane's thrust is being made by the pressure difference between the lower pressure air in front of the engine inlet and the higher pressure air behind the shock wave inside the engine inlet.

NASA photo

SHOCK WAVES

Supersonic air

Faster air means lower pressure

Slower air means higher pressure

Higher pressure air wants to move toward lower pressure area. This pulls the airplane forward

Rocket Engines

Whether they are pistons, turbines, ramjets or scramjets, most engines burn a mixture of fuel and air. But spacecraft fly where there is no air. So they need a different kind of engine. Rocket engines are used to get spacecraft into space because a rocket doesn't depend on outside air to burn. It carries everything it needs inside.

How Does a Rocket Engine Work?

A rocket engine carries its own fuel inside. That fuel can be solid or liquid. But it also carries something called an **oxidizer**. An oxidizer is whatever mixes with the fuel to make it burn. In air-breathing airplane engines, the oxidizer is air, which is brought into the engine from the outside. But since rocket engines are designed to work in space, where there is no air, they have to carry their oxidizer with them. The fuel and oxidizer mix in a combustion chamber, and the exhaust from that explosion is sent out the back of the rocket just like the exhaust of a jet engine.

Since Newton's third law of motion says that for every action, there is an opposite and equal reaction, the thrust going out the back of the rocket forces the rocket up in the air.

Early Astronaut and Satellite Rocket Engines

In the first days of human space flight, the astronauts sat in a small capsule on top of a long rocket. The rocket had several *stages*, each of which had its own engine that would fire, burn up its fuel, and then drop away from the rest of the rocket. The capsule itself had no big engines. The last rocket stage would put the capsule in orbit and then drop away. When the astronauts got ready to return to Earth, they would fire small braking rockets (similar to reaction control jets). These rockets would slow the capsule below the speed it needed to stay in orbit. The capsule would then start falling toward Earth, re-enter the atmosphere, and splash down under parachutes in one of the Earth's oceans.

A satellite works the same way. When a satellite is put into space, the satellite takes the place of the astronaut capsule in the nose cone of the rocket. The rocket drops away in stages, leaving the satellite in orbit.

NASA photo

The Space Shuttle

The Space Shuttle was the next step in rocket engine development, because parts of the Shuttle's engines were designed to be reusable. For launch, the Shuttle orbiter is mounted on a large main tank that holds the liquid fuel for the Shuttle's three main engines. On each side of that tank is a solid-fuel booster rocket that helps give the Shuttle extra thrust for lift off. When the solid booster rockets are empty, they drop off and splash down into the ocean under parachutes. The boosters can then be refilled and used again. The main tank puts the Shuttle into its orbit and then drops off. Eventually, as the tank falls, it burns up in the Earth's atmosphere.

Once the main tank is gone, the Shuttle is essentially a glider. It has little rocket motors called **reaction controls** that are fired to "steer" it in space (read more about reaction controls in the section on "Space Controls"). When the astronauts are ready to come back to Earth, the pilots turn the Shuttle around so that its tail is facing forward. They then fire a "maneuvering" rocket engine out of its tail. Since the tail is facing forward, that's like putting a jet engine in reverse. It slows the Shuttle down below orbital speed, which causes the Shuttle to drop toward the Earth's atmosphere. Once the Shuttle is back in the Earth's atmosphere, its pilots fly it back to a runway landing without power, just like a glider.

NASA photo

NASA photo

The AeroSpike Engine

The exhaust from most rockets goes through nozzles at the back end of the engine. If you watch a Space Shuttle launch on television, you'll see three nozzles underneath the Shuttle — one from each of its engines. These nozzles can point in different directions, a little like thrust-vectoring airplane engines. This is what steers the Shuttle (or any other rocket) in one direction or the other.

But NASA has also tested a new kind of rocket engine that might work better. It's called a Linear AeroSpike Rocket Engine. What makes it different is that it uses two streams of rocket exhaust shooting out the two sides of a curved center ramp instead of the standard "bell" shaped rocket nozzles. It's a lot

Real Life Profile: Student Space Scientists
DuVal High School, Lanham, MD

What would happen if a cockroach or two stowed away on a Space Shuttle mission to the International Space Station? Would the roaches die off quickly, or would the Space Station astronauts soon have a cosmic-sized pest problem?

This is the question a group of students at DuVal High School in Maryland set out to answer with their very own space science experiment. The local chapter of the American Institute of Aeronautics and Astronautics had bought them space in a GAS can on a Shuttle mission. GAS stands for "Get Away Special" experiments, which are trashcan-sized containers that fit into the Shuttle's cargo bay. And they're inexpensive enough that even schools can afford to send an experiment into space!

DuVal's Periplaneta Americana cockroaches rocketed into space in October 1998, with John Glenn. While only two of the roaches survived the trip, the school is trying to raise funds for a smaller follow-up mission to fix some problems that might have affected the outcome of the first experiment.

The X-33 research vehicle was designed to use a Linear AeroSpike Rocket Engine.

NASA photo

lighter than the heavy bell nozzles, and it can still make the rocket turn by changing how much exhaust is coming out each side of the ramp.

If this engine works as well as it's supposed to, it may be used on the spaceship that replaces the Space Shuttle!

Real Life Profile: Erica Robinson
15 years old, Aviation Explorer Scout, Student Pilot
Temecula, CA

Erica Robinson's dad is a pilot, but she didn't have much interest in flying until she got a lesson from a young, female flight instructor. "Her passion for it was contagious," Robinson says. "And I love the way it blocks your mind from everything else. You're totally there in the airplane, and it gives you this incredible feeling."

Robinson joined a local Aviation Explorer Scout troop, which is part of the Boy Scouts of America. Through the scout troop she has gotten additional flying time, tours of air museums and military airplanes, and the chance to work on the "line" at local air shows. Her scout troop is even offering a ground school course to help its 18 members work on their private pilot licenses.

Although she can't solo a plane for another year, Robinson has 15 hours of flight instruction. She pays for half the cost by doing chores and babysitting, and her parents pay the other half. Her goal? To become a commercial airline pilot.

Landing Gear

Another important part of an airplane's design is its landing gear. Just as different types of shoes let you do different sports (cleats, hockey skates, climbing crampons), different types of landing gear let airplanes do different jobs. And sometimes, those jobs are in really odd or remote places! Here are just a few different types of landing gear planes use.

Fixed Gear

A lot of small airplanes have what is called "fixed" landing gear. This means the plane's wheels stay down during the whole flight. There are two kinds of "fixed" gear airplanes. The early planes, and some sport planes still built today, are known as **conventional gear**, **tailwheel**, or **taildragger** airplanes. This is because they have two main wheels near the front of the plane and a little wheel at the back, or *tail*, of the airplane. This makes the plane sit at an angle with its nose pointing up in the air when it's sitting on the ground.

The other kind of fixed gear airplane is called a **nosewheel** or **tricycle gear** airplane, because its wheels are arranged like those on a tricycle. It has two main wheels and then a smaller wheel under its nose.

This 1940s Luscombe has "conventional" gear.

At one time almost all planes were taildraggers. Taildraggers are still very good for landing on grass or rough strips, since a small nosewheel has a greater chance of catching on something and flipping the airplane over on its back. A tailwheel can also create less drag than a nosewheel, since tailwheels tend to be smaller and closer to the fuselage than nosewheels.

The disadvantage to a tailwheel airplane is that it's harder to steer on the ground. Its center of gravity is behind its main gear, and its "steering" wheel is at the back. This combination makes it want to swap ends all the time. It's just like a shopping cart. If you've ever tried to push a shopping cart backwards, you know that it really wants to turn around. To steer it straight backwards, you have to almost "S" turn the cart back and forth, anticipating its next move. A tailwheel airplane acts the same way. And because its nose is up in the air, it can be harder to see what's in front of the airplane.

This Cessna 150 has "tricycle" gear.

Retractable Gear

Airplanes that are designed for speed need to reduce drag as much as possible. So faster airplanes — from a Mooney or Cessna 210 to an airliner or fighter jet — all have systems to pull up (retract) the gear into the airplane during the flight. While this creates less drag, retractable gear systems add extra weight and are one more thing that can break. (Lowering the gear for landing is also one more thing the pilot can accidentally forget, which is why most training airplanes don't have retractable gear!) So many cargo planes or "bush" airplanes have fixed gear, because speed is not as important as the airplane's weight, strength, durability and dependability.

Beech Bonanza.

Floats and Boats

What if you want to fly up to some remote lake to go fishing or take your airplane to a distant lagoon in the Caribbean? Wheels won't be as useful as **floats**. Some planes just have plain floats for landing gear. But then they *have* to land on the water. So some owners put **amphibious floats** on their planes. These are floats that have wheels tucked up alongside them, as well. The pilot can put the wheels down and land on a runway, or pull the wheels up and land with the floats on the water.

Of course, if you *really* wanted to land on that Caribbean lagoon, you might want to consider a **flying boat**. The bottom of a flying boat is shaped like the hull of a boat. So the main cabin of the plane lands in the water. Since the center of gravity on these planes is lower in the water, they tend to be more stable, which is better for landing where the water may be less calm than on a mountain lake.

Some flying boats are also amphibians. This Grumman Goose can put its wheels up and land in the water, or put its wheels down and land on a runway. Remember, though, that all these extra abilities cost money, and they add extra drag, equipment and weight to the airplane, which slows it down and lets it carry less. So you have to decide what is more important — a plane that can fly faster, or one that can land in the water!

Grumman Goose.

Skis/Wheel-Skis

Anyone who's spent much time in Minnesota, North Dakota or Alaska knows that it's snowy there 4-6 months out of the year. The lakes freeze over — and so do some of the small runways. In these places, pilots often trade in their wheels or floats for skis in the wintertime. As with floats, skis come in two varieties. Some planes have plain skis for landing gear, which means the pilot has to land on ice or snow. Other planes have wheel-skis, which are like amphibious floats. The pilot can retract the skis above the wheels and land on a runway, or extend the skis and land on the snow. With skis on a plane, pilots can land on glaciers, frozen lakes, or just

Photo courtesy of EAA

about any snow-covered field. But skis don't have any brakes to help the plane slow down. So skiplane landings can be a real challenge!

Helicopter Landing Gear

Designers of helicopters also need to think about where the helicopter needs to land. Most helicopters have skids, which are solid tubes of metal that touch down on the pavement. But some helicopters are designed to land on the water. Since helicopters can land vertically, they don't need floats that can cut through the water. Instead, they use pontoons (like a pontoon boat) that sit on top of the water and let the helicopter float.

Tundra Tires

What if you REALLY want to rough it? What if you want to be a bush pilot in Alaska and land on rocky gravel bars and rough mountain meadows? Or you have to go track gazelles across the Serengeti of Africa, landing in bumpy, out-of-the-way clearings and on rutted, dirt roads? You'll need some serious off-road tires, or **tundra tires**, as they're known in the flying world. Tundra tires are huge, so they won't get stuck in ruts and are less likely to get caught on rocks. (Think about rolling a huge playground ball across a rocky surface versus a small superball. Which one is more likely to roll over the rocks without getting stuck?)

Of course, these tires create a lot of drag, so you have to decide what's most important — speed or the ability to land in rough places. It's hard to have both.

Photo courtesy of EAA

This Sherpa plane has bigger than normal tundra tires.

NASA photo

Skids

The early airplanes aren't the only planes that ever used skids for landing gear. The X-15 used metal skids for its main gear because its designers couldn't figure out how to protect rubber tires at the extremely high temperatures the X-15 would have to stand. (This is also why the Space Shuttle's tires are so small.) The X-15 also needed very sturdy gear, since the plane touched down at over 200 miles an hour. The designers knew the X-15 would only land on lakebeds and under very controlled conditions. So they decided to use skids instead of wheels on the plane's main gear. The skids would be easier to build and would help slow the plane down as the skids dragged across the lakebed surface.

Real Life Profile: Will Sherman
Bush Pilot, Gakona, AK

Will Sherman is younger than a lot of the old seasoned bush pilots in Alaska. But he's still seen more adventures than most pilots in the lower 48 states.

In the winter, he puts skis on his Super Cub airplane and flies off glaciers, frozen lakes and snow fields. Come spring, he puts 30" tundra tires on his plane and flies off remote Alaskan beaches, spotting fish for commercial fishermen.

In the summer, he becomes a ferry pilot and guide, taking supplies, hunters, mountain climbers, private fishermen and other backwoods adventurers into the remote Alaskan wilderness. Most of the time, he doesn't even have a dirt runway to land on. He lands in all sorts of short spaces, including beaches, gravel bars in rivers, and open sections of tundra.

"To make a living as a bush pilot you have to do a lot of different things," he explains. And yet he takes it all in stride.

"People in other places might think the kind of flying I do is unusual," Sherman says. "But up here, this stuff is just everyday flying."

Construction Materials

One of the other main things you need to consider in designing an airplane is what materials to use in actually building it. When airplanes were first invented, there weren't a lot of choices in materials. But today there are lots of options. Which one or ones you choose depends on what you want the airplane to do. In fact, a plane's outside skin, or material, can tell you a lot about the airplane's abilities.

Photo courtesy of EAA

Fabric and Wood

The early airplanes were almost all wood frames covered in fabric. Wood is simple to form, easy to work with, and lightweight. Fabric could be easily formed to the wood to provide a cover and a solid airfoil. The fabric was then coated with a paint-like compound called **dope** to make the fabric stiff and strong. As time went on, some airplane fuselages were made out of steel tubes instead of wood, since steel was more durable, but they were still covered in fabric.

Today, there are still a lot of small airplanes made out of steel tube or wood and fabric. Most of them are "homebuilt" planes — planes built by individual people in their garages or hangars, as opposed to planes built by big companies. There are some companies that still build steel tube and fabric planes. But the fabric that people use now is a synthetic polyester Dacron, which is much stronger, safer and easier to use than cotton.

The advantage of a fabric airplane is that it's fairly easy and quick to build, and it's lightweight. One advantage of a lightweight plane is that it will land in a shorter distance than a heavy plane. So lots of small airplanes built to land in short bush strips, like Maules or Huskys, are made of fabric. But fabric airplanes can't withstand high speeds. So if you see an airplane covered in fabric, you know it was designed to be lightweight or easy to build, not fast.

Aluminum

Most airplanes today are built of aluminum, whether they are small training planes or big airliners. The surface of aluminum planes can be made fairly smooth, and aluminum can withstand speeds up above Mach 2. So it's very versatile material for building airplanes.

Photo courtesy of Cessna Aircraft Company

Real Life Profile: Shop Class With Wings
**Central Kitsap Junior High School
Silverdale, WA**

Some shop classes build electric lights or wood sculptures. But one of Steve Smith's shop classes is building an airplane. A local pilot offered to buy the plans and materials for a Zenith CH 701 — a simple aluminum airplane that the students would have to build from scratch.

Other local pilots have joined in the effort. Two days a week the students and pilots work side-by-side for several hours, riveting metal, forming and assembling pieces, and talking about flying and adventures yet to come.

The students get class credit for their work. But the real reward will come when the plane is finished. The students will then have an airplane in which they can learn to fly.

Photo courtesy of EAA

Composites

Since the 1970s, people have also begun building planes out of **composite** materials. The phrase "composite" actually doesn't refer to a specific material, but a type of construction. One kind of "composite," for example, might have a foam core sandwiched in between two layers of fiberglass. Since the surface is made of more than one material, designers started calling that kind of construction "composite," meaning a mix of two or more things.

One advantage of composite construction materials is that they make it easier for an airplane builder to make complex curves. Why? Because composite wings don't start as one solid piece. Builders lay strips of fiberglass fabric one on top of another, like wrapping an ace bandage around an ankle. They can twist, turn, and layer the fiberglass (or carbon fiber) in all sorts of creative ways. For this reason, odd and new types of wing or fuselage curve shapes are easier to make with composite materials than they would be with aluminum. The Nemesis racer's unique wing shape (shown in the "Fast Wings" section), for example, would have been harder to make if the racer was an aluminum plane.

Composite wings are also easier to make very smooth, since they don't need screws or rivets to hold the aluminum skin to an inner structure. As a result, they are very good for creating fast, slick, "laminar flow" wings. Composite materials also can be very good for military planes, because they are harder to see on radar.

Mylar (gossamer wings)

The planes called "gossamer" airplanes are really fabric airplanes. But the plastic material they use to cover their wings — which is similar to the material used in the silver "Happy Birthday" balloons you can buy in a store — is a very special kind of fabric. It's designed for one purpose only: light weight. It's not very sturdy, so it can't stand strong winds, abrupt movements, or anything but slow-speed flight. But if you want a plane light enough to power by your own leg power, or a plane light enough to fly to 70,000 feet on tiny, solar-powered motors, this mylar covering is just about the lightest-weight fabric you can cover an airplane in and still create lift. Or at least it's the lightest-weight fabric we know of now. New materials are being developed all the time!

NASA photos

Titanium

Titanium is a very lightweight, strong metal that withstands heat much better than aluminum. The only problems with it are that it's very expensive and it's difficult to work with. So designers save titanium for airplanes that absolutely have to be very resistant to heat. The SR-71 is made of titanium, for example, because its designers knew that at Mach 3, some places on the airplane would be as hot as 1,000 degrees!

Neat Fact

The SR-71 gets so hot when it flies that it actually stretches! It's almost a foot longer at its top speed than it is on the ground!

Inconel X

Inconel X is a very rare alloy, or mixture of metals, that is *extremely* good at withstanding heat. The X-15 was built out of Inconel X because it was designed to fly 6 times the speed of sound! And at high speed, the air molecules are screaming past the airplane, scraping along its wings, fuselage and tail. That movement across the skin of the airplane causes friction. And as anyone who's ever gotten a friction burn on a gym floor knows, friction causes heat. So the faster the speed, the more heat the airplane has to be able to stand.

Neat Fact

In 1967, the X-15 set a speed record over 4,000 miles an hour! But even Inconel X couldn't withstand the heat at that speed. Even with a white, heat-resistant coating the airplane still came back with holes burned through parts of it — all caused by the friction heat of how fast it had flown!

Supersonic Plane Design

What if you have a supersonic need for speed? Pedal to the metal, as fast as you can go, Mach 2 with your hair on fire? If you want to build a plane that can beat its own sound to wherever it's going, there are a few things you'd better consider. The rules change as you get close to the speed of sound.

Shock Waves

Air behaves like water in many ways — even at high speeds. Imagine a boat powering slowly through the water. The movement of the boat will send ripples or waves through the water ahead of it. If the boat isn't moving very fast, the ripples will stay ahead of the boat. But if the boat picks up speed, it will soon catch up with the ripples. The water can't move as fast as the boat is speeding. This actually makes it harder for the boat to make progress through the water. Why? Because the water is already kind of making way for the boat if ripples are opening up ahead of it. But when the boat outspeeds the ripples, it has to force its way through water that's not moving.

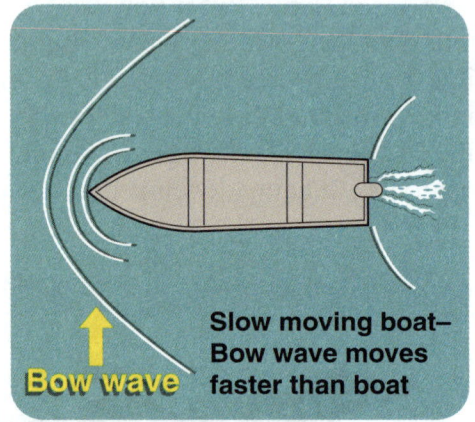
Slow moving boat— Bow wave moves faster than boat

The same thing happens with an airplane. If it's moving slower than the speed of sound, its movement will send ripples through the air in front of it. But if the plane goes faster than those ripples can travel through the air, it runs into a kind of "barrier" where, in a sense, the air starts being "shocked" by the movement of the plane. The abrupt changes this causes in the air and its pressure are what cause the **sonic boom** noise we hear on the ground when an airplane above us goes faster than sound. These changes also affect how the airplane flies.

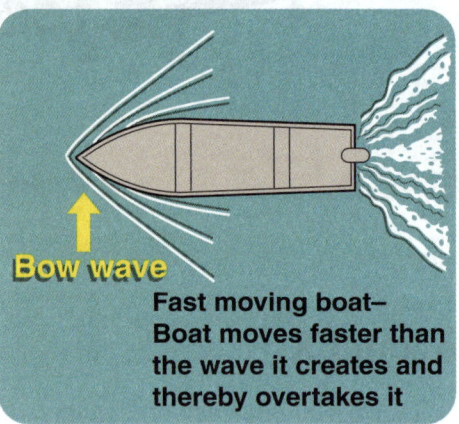
Fast moving boat— Boat moves faster than the wave it creates and thereby overtakes it

Supersonic Airplane Design

The shock waves created by an airplane as it approaches the speed of sound cause some unique design problems. The bigger and more blunt the frontal area of the plane is, the more effort it will take to force its way through the air. A slender nose may be able to cut its way through the air okay, but when the wings hit that barrier, it's like a diver hitting the water spread-eagled instead of with his arms tight alongside his body. But airplanes need wings to fly. So what can be done to solve this problem?

For one thing, a NASA engineer named Richard Whitcomb figured out that if you made the plane's fuselage narrower where the wings were, it would help reduce the amount of frontal surface that had to be forced through the air. Look at photos of most supersonic jets, and you'll see that their fuselages are narrower where their wings are.

Supersonic wings usually have what engineers call a **low aspect ratio**, which means they're short and wide (as opposed to long and narrow, like the wings of a glider). Supersonic wings also tend to be thin and swept, with sharp leading edges and only a slight camber, or curve, in them. All of these things help the wing cut through the air without causing such a big shock wave.

Supersonic Control Surfaces

The shock waves caused by a plane flying faster than sound also affect the kind of control surfaces the plane has to have. The shock wave coming off the back side of the wing can cause a severe "buffeting" on the plane's elevator, which can send the plane out of control. So supersonic planes all have all-moving **stabilators** instead of fixed horizontal tails with moving **elevators**. The *whole horizontal surface* of a supersonic plane's tail moves up and down.

NASA photo

Neat Fact
Even a Boeing 747 airliner uses Whitcomb's design approach. Instead of making the fuselage narrower where the wing is, its designers created a big bump ahead of where the wings are — so there's not such a big jump in frontal area from the nose to the wings. This is why 747s have a second story at the front of the airplane! It may seem odd to make an airplane's nose *bigger* in order to make the plane go faster but like we said, the rules change near the speed of sound.

Neat Fact
Captain Charles "Chuck" Yeager learned about controlling a supersonic plane the hard way. The X-1 he flew to break the sound barrier was designed with a normal elevator. But when he got close to Mach 1, the plane went out of control. He got control back when the plane slowed down again. On future flights, he controlled the plane at high speeds by "trimming," or adjusting, the whole horizontal stabilizer up or down. But his flights showed designers that they needed to put an all-moving horizontal on any supersonic plane.

Photo courtesy of The Boeing Company

Slowing Down a Supersonic Plane

Once you design a plane to go as fast as it possibly can, you only have one problem left. At some point, it has to slow down enough to land on a reasonable length runway. And the faster you make the plane's wing and design, the tougher it's going to be to slow it down.

One way designers solve this problem is giving supersonic planes **drag chutes**. A drag chute is a parachute that shoots out behind an airplane after it lands and creates a lot of...you guessed it...**drag**. That slows the airplane down.

But a drag chute isn't practical for an airliner. So what would you do to slow down a supersonic airliner? Look at the Russian Tu-144. It has a delta wing, which is an excellent design for high speed cruise flight. But delta wings don't have flaps, which most airplanes use to slow down. So where does that leave planes like the Tu-144 or the Concorde? They've got Mach 2 wings, and they can't even use flaps to increase the **camber** (curve) of their wings to create more lift at slower speeds or slow down. The only way an SST can create more lift or slow down is to increase the wing's **angle of attack**. This is why the Tu-144 and Concorde come in to land with their noses so high in the air. But there's a problem with this, too. With the nose that high, the pilots can't see where they're going. The solution? The Tu-144 and Concorde have hinged noses that can "droop" down for take off and landing. This allows the pilots to see.

Virtual Reality Cockpit

The next kind of supersonic airliner may have a better idea than a droop nose to let the pilots see where they're going. Thanks to virtual reality and remote camera technology, the supersonic airliner of the 21st century might not have cockpit windows at all! Its pilots might have images of the real runway or a "virtual" runway projected on screens in front of them, instead.

NASA's Record-Setting Supersonic Airplanes

NASA photos

The X-1: First plane to break the sound barrier and fly supersonic (Air Force and NASA).

The X-15: Set an airplane speed record of Mach 6.7 (over 4,000 miles an hour).

The D-558-2 Skyrocket: Another early experimental rocket plane flown by pilots at Dryden. It was the first plane to go Mach 2 (two times the speed of sound).

The SR-71: First plane powered by air-breathing engines to go over Mach 3. (Built by Lockheed, now flown by NASA.)

Putting It Together

If you were looking at a basic recipe for an airplane, it might look something like this:
Ingredients:
1. Wings
2. Stability and Control Surfaces
3. Engines
4. Landing Gear
5. Construction materials and covering

Airplane designers are kind of like chefs. They look at these basic ingredients that every airplane has to have and select specific types of wings, engines, etc., depending on what kind of job they want the airplane to do. Then they mix and match, modify and mold, until they have a design that does what they want it to do and is still safe and practical to fly.

Before you set off to design your own plane, take a second look at some of the masters' designs. Think about what you've read so far — what a swept wing does, what a straight, long and narrow wing does, what an oblique or swing wing does, and what a flexible wing does. Think about when a jet engine makes more sense than a piston, or when fabric is a good covering for an airplane. When would floats be worth the extra drag they create? Are big flaps important? How about a canard?

Now look at some of these photos closely and see if you can tell, by the kind of wings, engines, control surfaces, coverings, and gear they have, what they were designed to do well.

AASI Aircraft

Jetcruzer
This AASI Jetcruzer has a single turboprop engine with a pusher propeller (propeller at the back). It has a forward canard and a slightly swept wing further back on the plane. The wing has a very unusual leading edge, because the outer part of it droops down lower than the inside portion. The wing is also very smooth. The plane has retractable gear and a big cabin that can seat 6 or 8 people.

NASA photo

NASA F-18
The F-18 Hornet has two jet engines with afterburners. It has a thin swept wing with a low aspect ratio (short and wide), with flaps and speed brakes. It has retractable gear, and is built out of aluminum and composites.

NASA photo

NASA photo

NASA ER-2
This ER-2 has very long, high-aspect ratio (long and narrow) wings. It has a single jet engine, and a very narrow fuselage and cockpit. It has conventional control surfaces, except its ailerons are very long, just like its wing. But it has very unusual landing gear. Instead of main wheels placed next to each other, its main wheels are like those on a bicycle — one behind the other. The plane also has two little wheels under each wingtip that drop away when it takes off.

NASA Space Shuttle
The Space Shuttle has thick wings with very rounded front edges. They are swept, and covered by thermal protective tiles. The Shuttle is a delta wing design, with elevons (no flaps) on the trailing edge of the wing for pitch and roll control. It has three rocket engines, but it doesn't use them when it lands. It has a rudder that splits to act as a speed brake, and has a drag chute that deploys after it touches down. It also has tiny little landing gear.

Photo courtesy of Cessna Aircraft Company

Ag Plane
This Cessna AgWagon crop dusting plane has straight, thick wings with a very big curve (or **camber**). Its braced wings make it strong and able to carry a large load of fertilizer or insecticide. It has a spray bar across the back side of its wing to distribute these chemicals over crops. It has regular, basic control surfaces, very sturdy fixed gear with big tires, and a powerful piston engine.

Put It Together Yourself!

Now that you know a lot about what different ingredients let an airplane do, you're ready to start playing chef yourself! As a warm-up, look at these different combinations of wings, engines, control surfaces, landing gear and coverings, and see if you can tell what an airplane with these parts could do well.

Photo courtesy of EAA

Piper Cub ingredients:

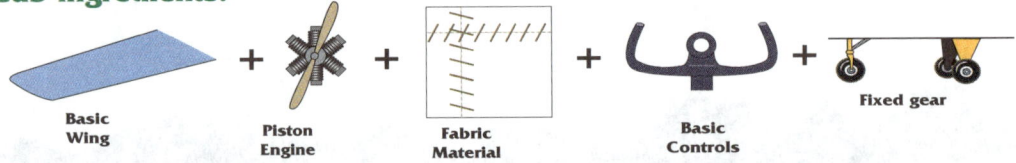

Basic Wing + Piston Engine + Fabric Material + Basic Controls + Fixed gear

Real Life Profile: Phillip Lockwood
Pilot and Aircraft Designer, Leza Lockwood, Inc.
Sebring, FL

When a National Geographic photographer needed a plane that he could use to track and shoot pictures of animals in the remote African rainforest, he called designer and pilot Phil Lockwood. Lockwood's answer was the "AirCam."

The Air Cam is extremely light, so it can be carried into remote areas easily. It can also take off in as little as 80 feet and flies slowly and quietly enough that it doesn't scare the animals the photographers want to shoot. Lockwood also designed the plane to have two engines, because the rainforest is not a good place for an emergency landing.

What else makes it a great National Geographic photo plane? The AirCam is also built to let photographers sit up front in the open air, so they can shoot photos at any angle.

The X-31's ingredients:

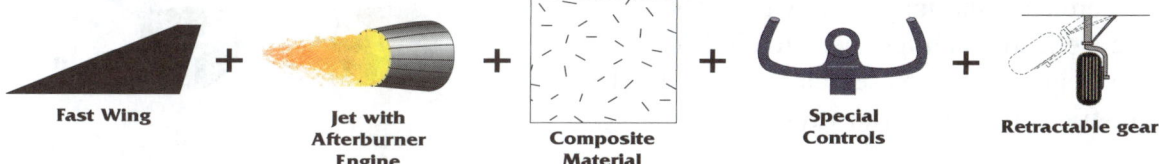

What Could These Airplanes Do?

Now, just looking at these icons, see if you can figure out what a plane with these general characteristics could do well.

Airplane #1 ingredients:

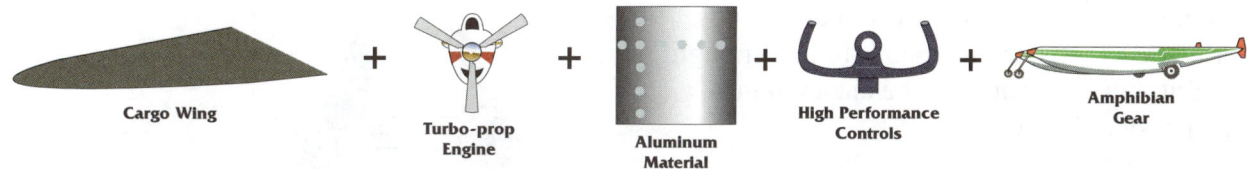

Airplane #2 ingredients:

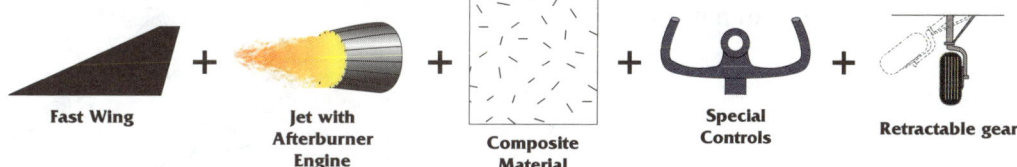

Design It Yourself!

Now do what every other designer does. Start with the mission you want your plane to do. Maybe you're on a secret rescue mission to the Andes mountains of South America. You have to fly in through the high mountain passes, then land on a short rocky cliff 10,000 feet in the air to pick up three resistance fighters trapped behind enemy lines. There might not be any fuel there, so you have to carry enough fuel to get there and back. You also may be pursued on your way out, so you need a plane that's either fast or able to hide and maneuver around the rocky mountainsides.

Or maybe you're tracking the elusive Wildebeest through the Serengeti and jungles of Africa. These animals hide well, so you might need to circle or hover over one spot while you search for them. Fuel is scarce in Africa, and paved runways are even scarcer.

Maybe your mission is a quick response dash to the middle of Russia to deliver a rare antidote to a deadly poison that has infected 1,000 people and threatens to spread to the rest of the world. It's 10,000 miles away, and every minute counts. But there's a catch. The runway at the town is only 3,000 feet long (this is very short for any jet).

Or maybe you just want a plane you can fit in your garage and pull out on the weekends and go for a little hop around the patch with your best friends. You want it to do loops and rolls and fly fast enough to be fun. But you also want it to be cheap, lightweight, and easy to build.

From whatever mission you choose, start going through all the different wings, engines, control surfaces, construction materials, landing gear, and special high-performance possibilities an airplane can have, and figure out what combination might get your job done!

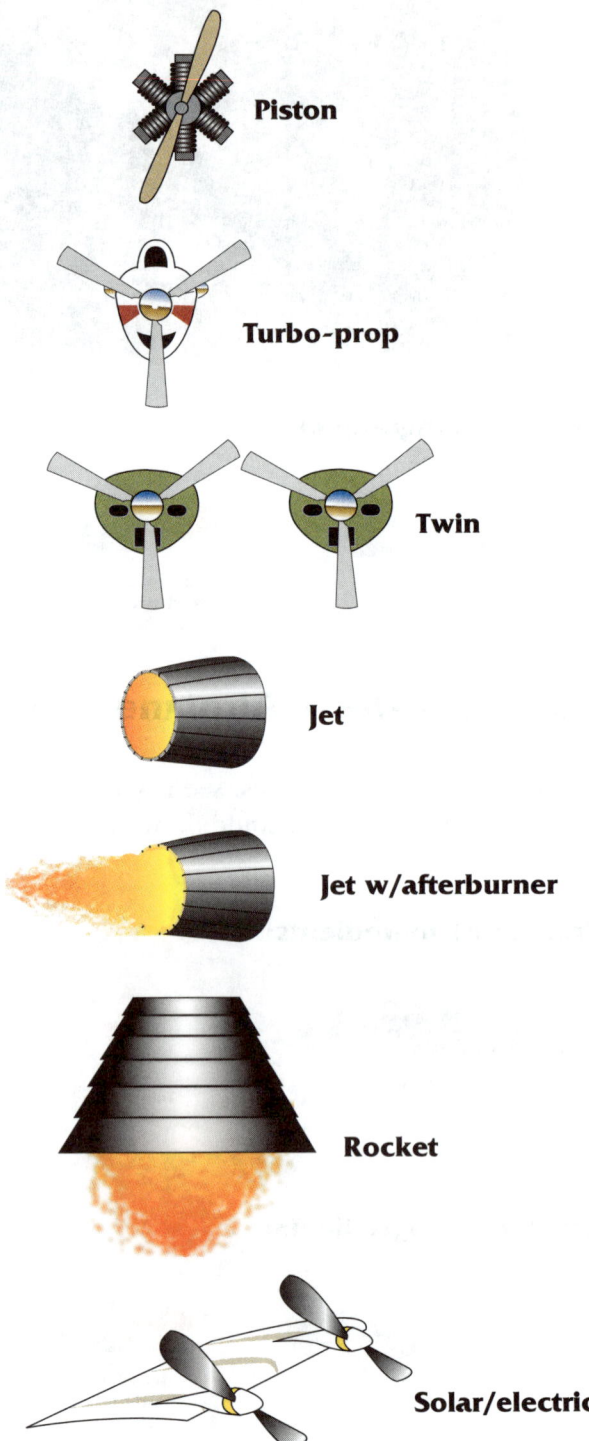

Engines

Piston

Turbo-prop

Twin

Jet

Jet w/afterburner

Rocket

Solar/electric

Wings

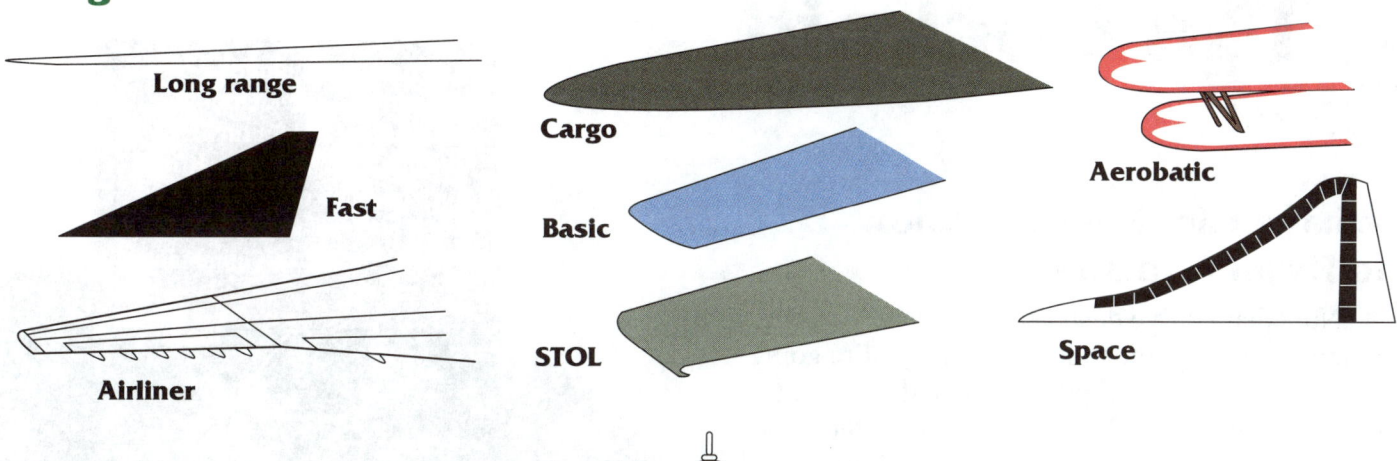

Materials

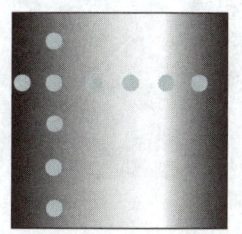

Aluminum

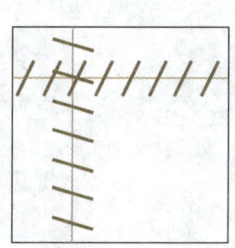

Fabric

Wood

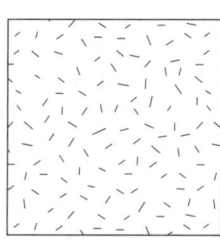

Composite

Controls

Basic — High Performance — Special — Space

Gear

Fixed gear — Tundra tires — Retractable gear

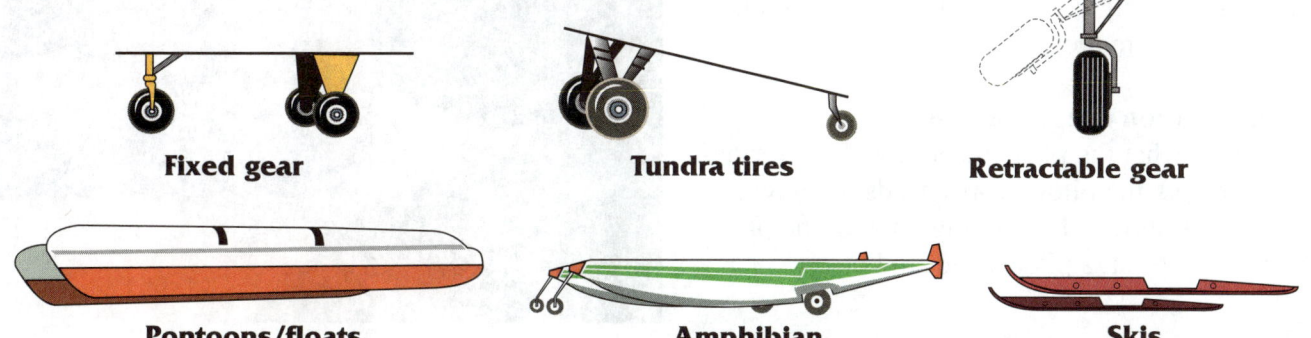

Pontoons/floats — Amphibian — Skis

The Cockpit

What a Pilot Needs to Know to Fly an Airplane

Now that you've designed the outside of your dream plane, it's time to look at what you're going to put INSIDE the cockpit — that is, if you want anyone to be able to fly it. The basics are the same whether the plane is a tiny glider or the Space Shuttle. A more complex airplane may add other things to the basic instruments and controls, and the displays may be more complicated, but the basic controls and information a pilot needs are the same.

What does a pilot need? First, she or he needs a way to move the control surfaces of the airplane. In most airplanes, the pilot has a control yoke or control stick, which is linked to the ailerons and elevators. Turn or push the yoke/stick to the right, and the plane will roll to the right. Turn the yoke to the left, and the plane will roll left. Pull back and the nose will come up; push forward and the nose will go down. The pilot also has rudder pedals, which are connected (as you might guess) to the rudder. Push on the left rudder pedal, and the rudder moves to the left. Push on the right one, and it moves to the right. The rudder pedals also usually have brakes attached to them. Most planes are set up so that a pilot can press on the top part of the rudder pedal to apply the brake.

Pilots also have a **throttle** to control how much power the engine is making, and levers or switches to turn on the fuel and ignition systems. More complicated planes will also have levers to put the flaps and gear up and down, open or close speed brakes or slats, and in some cases, adjust the propeller settings. Airliners, fighter jets, and high-performance airplanes will have even more switches and levers. But these are the basics.

What information does a pilot need?

No matter what the plane is, or how the information is presented, the pilot always needs to know a few basic facts about what's going on with the plane.

At the very least, a pilots needs to know:

1. How fast the plane is going. The **airspeed indicator** says how fast (in either knots or miles per hour) the plane is flying.

3. Whether the plane is straight and level, climbing, descending, or in a turn. An **attitude indicator**, or **artificial horizon**, shows whether the wings are level or in a turn and whether the plane is climbing or descending.

4. Whether the controls are all "coordinated." A **turn and bank indicator** has a needle that shows if the plane's wings are *banked*, or in a turn, and a bubble, like in a carpenter's level, that shows if the rudder and aileron controls are coordinated, or in agreement with each other.

Cirrus SR-20

2. How high the plane is flying. The **altimeter** (short for "altitude meter") tells a pilot the plane's *altitude* — or how high it is above sea level.

5. How much power the engine is making. A **tachometer** tells how fast the propeller is turning in "revolutions per minute," or RPMs. **Oil temperature** and **oil pressure** gauges help the pilot keep track of what's going on with the engine.

6. Where the airplane is going. A **compass** (or directional gyro) gives a pilot basic information about what direction the airplane is flying.

The Airliner Cockpit

This Boeing 767 cockpit looks a whole lot more complicated than the Cirrus SR-20's cockpit. Like most newer airliners, a lot of its important information is presented on computer-like screens called **electronic flight displays**. The panel also has numerous other gauges, switches and levers. But believe it or not, the instruments in this panel give the pilot the same basic information as the few round instruments in the SR-20.

1. The Primary Flight Display. This top screen has *airspeed* information on one side, *altitude* information on the other, and *attitude* information in the center. But just in case the plane has an electrical failure, gauges with this same information are also put on the instrument panel. The back-up *airspeed indicator*, *altimeter* and *compass* are just like the instruments in the Cub.

2. The Horizontal Situation Indicator (HSI) display. This is kind of a "moving map" display that tells the pilot *where the airplane is going*. Unlike the Piper Cub's compass, however, this display can also show the pilot how to steer the plane to get it where she or he wants to go. A pilot can just follow the HSI's dotted lines or put the plane on *autopilot* and let the plane's flight computer automatically follow the right path to whatever destination the pilot has chosen. The back-up HSI on the panel looks a lot like a compass, but it's more accurate and can be hooked up to the plane's autopilot.

3. Engine Instruments. This middle screen shows the pilots what is going on with the airliner's two engines. These displays tell the pilots what the *RPM* and *temperature* levels are for each of the engines. This information lets the pilots know if the engines are okay, and how much more thrust the engines can create. The panel also contains back-up mechanical RPM and engine temperature instruments, in case the electronic displays break.

4. Flight Management System Keypad. This keypad is how the pilots program the plane's flight computer, which is sometimes called a flight management system. This computer runs the autopilot, sets up navigation courses, and puts different types of information up on the panel's computer screens. The pilots type in their commands to the computer on this calculator-type keypad.

What are all the other switches?

An airliner has a lot more systems and parts than a small Piper Cub or SR-20 does. An airliner has inside and outside lights and beacons, oxygen and pressurization systems, air conditioning, fuel pumps, hydraulic pumps, heating systems for all sorts of different parts of the plane, and lots of other smaller bells and whistles. In addition to flying the plane, the pilots have to watch and control all these other things, as well. That's why there are so many switches in an airliner's cockpit.

The Fighter Cockpit

This McDonnell Douglas F-18 "Hornet" cockpit looks complicated. But these high-tech instruments are still giving the pilot the same basic information as the gauges in the Cirrus SR-20. It's just presented differently.

1. The Heads-Up Display (HUD). This is the primary flight display for an F-18 pilot. Information about *altitude*, *attitude*, *airspeed*, and *compass heading*, among other things, are all projected on this piece of clear glass. This way the pilot can keep looking out the window for enemy fighters while keeping track of what his instruments are telling him.

Small, back-up "mechanical" instruments that show this same information are located on the lower right-hand part of the instrument panel. Airplane designers generally include mechanical back-up instruments for electronic displays so pilots can still get the really important information they need even if the electrical displays break.

2. The Horizontal Situation Indicator (HSI). The center Multi-Function Display (MFD) can show different information. In this photo, it's showing system information, but it is generally used to display course information and a moving map. This map and course information tells the pilot where the plane is, where it's headed, and where it SHOULD be headed to get to whatever destination the pilot has chosen.

3. Multi-Function Displays (MFDs) or Digital Display Indicators (DDIs). These are the two computer screens on the left and right side of the instrument panel. The pilot can put all sorts of different information up on these screens, which is why they're sometimes called "multi-function" displays. They can display infrared or radar information about enemy targets or weather, engine information, weapons information, or the attitude of the airplane.

4. The "Up Front Control" Keypad. This numerical keypad is the main way the pilot can program the plane's navigation system or change what's on the different electronic displays in the cockpit. The keypad was put at the top of the panel so the pilot wouldn't have to look down in the cockpit to change the information on his screens. There are also several buttons on the control stick which allow the pilot to change and fire weapons and work some of the airplane's systems. These control stick buttons are another way the designers try to keep the fighter pilot's eyes outside the cockpit.

The Space Shuttle Cockpit

The Space Shuttle goes into space and flies 25 times the speed of sound (more than 18,000 miles per hour). But to bring it back to Earth safely, its Commander and Pilot still need the basic information every other pilot needs.

The Shuttle Commander (who flies in the left seat) and Pilot (who flies in the right seat) can program their displays to show different information in different places. But the typical display arrangement is:

1. Airspeed and Horizontal Situation Indicator. The two main computer displays in front of the Commander and Pilot show their basic flight information. The round circle on the Commander's left-hand screen is the Horizontal Situation Indicator (HSI). The HSI tells the pilots where the Shuttle is going (like a compass) and whether the Shuttle is on course. The rectangular boxes on the display show airspeed-related information.

2. Attitude and Altitude. The round circle on the right-hand display in front of the Commander shows what the attitude of the Shuttle is (whether it's level, in a turn, nose up, or nose down). The rectangular boxes on the right side of the display give information information on how high the Shuttle is and how fast it's climbing or descending. This is important, because the Shuttle has to glide from a re-entry point 4,200 miles away from the runway, and it only has one chance to make a landing.

3. Center Computer Screens. The five computer screens in the middle of the panel can be set up to show different types of information. For example, the top three displays here are showing information on some of the Shuttle's many complicated systems, and the display on the lower left is showing information about the Shuttle's engines.

4. Center Console Keypads. Between the Commander and Pilot are the controls for the Shuttle's navigation and computer systems. This is where the pilots can type in commands or changes.

5. Throttle. The Shuttle uses throttle-controllable rocket engines to get into space. So the pilots have a throttle, and the computer displays show them information about the temperature and power settings of the engines. The engines have no RPM setting or reading, because a rocket engine doesn't have moving parts. It's just thrust.

6. What are all the other switches? This photo is a close-up view of the Shuttle's main instrument panel. But the cockpit contains a lot more gauges, buttons, and switches. In fact, the Shuttle has so many systems to monitor and control that the cockpit has more than **2,000** buttons and switches in it!

Flying Outside The Plane

What if a plane has no cockpit? How do you fly it? If you've ever flown a radio-controlled model — or even played with a remote-controlled toy car — you know. You're still the pilot. You just stand on the ground instead of sitting in the cockpit. And you still need to control the plane's engine and control surfaces. Most simple radio-controlled airplanes have a hand-held box with two joysticks on them. Depending on how complex the model is (how many radio channels it has between the control box and the plane), you'll have more or less to control. The left joystick may control the rudder (left and right) and the engine throttle (up and down). The right joystick will typically control the ailerons (left and right) and the elevator (up and down).

Simple radio-controlled model planes don't give you any flight instruments. To tell what the plane is doing, you have to look up in the air and watch the plane itself. But NASA uses a lot of models in flight testing different ideas, and even some full-scale airplanes are built to be remote-controlled. Some of these planes have much more detailed control systems.

A Lakebed Cockpit

One of the lifting body plane designs tested at Dryden was a sleek radio-controlled model called the Hyper III. Since the Hyper III was more complex than most models, the researchers built a full ground cockpit for the pilot who flew it. The cockpit on the ground was hooked by radio signal to the plane. The ground cockpit had a control stick and flight instruments that told the pilot how fast and high the plane was flying, where it was headed, and what its attitude was. But the lakebed cockpit also let the pilot see the plane as it came in for a landing, which helped him control the landing much better.

Real Life Profile: Daniel Goldberg

**18 years old, Radio Controlled Airplane Model Race Pilot
Maui, HI**

Daniel Goldberg may be only 18 years old, but he's already a veteran air racer. He races giant scale airplanes – radio controlled race planes that are quarter to third-scale replicas of the real-life airplanes that compete at the Reno National Air Races. "It's a real adrenaline rush," he says. "There isn't the risk of getting hurt yourself, but you're still flying these racers at 200 – 240 miles an hour."

The Giant Scale Air Racing is the "top fuel" class in models, but most small model clubs around the country host air races for smaller, inexpensive radio controlled airplanes.

Goldberg's been racing five years and has already won a number of races. Eventually, he wants to get a regular pilot's license. But in the meantime, he's learning a lot just by building and flying his models. "I've flown 40 different kinds of model planes, and they all fly differently," he explains. "And even if it's a model, you still have to know how to land it in an emergency."

The Pathfinder/Centurion

The high-altitude Pathfinder and Centurion planes flight tested at Dryden are both remote-controlled airplanes. They require careful piloting, so the test pilots flying them on the ground are given a lot of information. Sometimes, the Pathfinder is flown by a pilot at a remote ground station, using instruments and controls that are linked by radio signal to the plane up in the air. But a pilot can also fly the Pathfinder from ground controls in a van. This van lets the ground pilot drive out to where the plane is going to land and land the plane by actually watching what it's doing instead of relying on remote images.

Real Life Profile: Tony Frackowiak
NASA Model Builder
NASA Dryden Flight Research Center, Edwards, CA

Tony Frackowiak's been building model airplanes all his life. The only difference is that now he gets paid for it. Tony is the primary model builder at NASA's Dryden Flight Research Center. He designs and builds models that allow engineers to test different concepts and designs.

Frackowiak's models range in size from 12-18" planes to planes that are 1/4 the size of an actual airplane. All of his models fly. Some are dropped from a radio-controlled "mothership" that has a wingspan of 10 feet and weighs 25 pounds.

Frackowiak says that he got a lot of information about model planes and radio control airplane clubs from his local hobby shop. From there, it was just a matter of pursuing it. "The trick is to find something you love and then figure out how to get paid for it," he says. "That's what I've done."

The Sky's The Limit

From the Wright brothers who designed the first powered plane, to the Rutan brothers who designed the first powered plane to go around the world non-stop, flight has been made possible by people who had the imagination to try something different.

What could you design? What kind of plane could you fly? What combination of materials, wings and control systems could you imagine that would make a plane nobody has ever made or flown before? Look at the incredible range of shapes and wings that airplane designers have already used to build better or different planes. Some are ugly, some are beautiful. Some are fast, some are slow. But each one was designed to do a specific job.

Now that you have a better idea of what different airplane parts do, and what designs are better for speed, maneuverability, or carrying a lot, try your own hand at designing the planes of the future! Think of a mission or job you might want an airplane to do — from lifting off from your back yard to chasing aliens through the galaxy. Then get out a pencil and paper and start figuring out how it needs to be designed.

Once, the sky was the limit. But we have planes that can reach into space, and new materials and systems are being developed all the time. Soon, the only limit will be what your imagination can dream. So let your imagination go, spread your wings, and FLY!!!

137

WILD BLUE WONDERS

Now that you know so much more about flying and designing airplanes, what can you do with all that information?

There are lots of ways to get involved in aviation, even as a kid or teenager. The Resource Guide at the back of this book lists a number of organizations that can help you, and there are always pilots at your local airport who would be more than happy to help you get closer to your dream of flight.

But the EAA's Wild Blue Wonders program is another way you can do something in and out of your school classroom that will help you learn and practice more about flight while having a really good time!

What is Wild Blue Wonders?

Wild Blue Wonders is a program sponsored by the EAA's Aviation Foundation in conjunction with aviation and aerospace museums around the country. It allows students to explore different aspects of flight through classroom activities or regional and national team competitions. Wild Blue Wonders uses aviation to help students master math, science and technology principles that will help them open doors to an aviation hobby or career.

Wild Blue Wonders teams are made up of five students and an advisor. When the team registers with EAA's Wild Blue Wonders office, it receives a flight kit with materials the team will need to hone its competition skills and achieve its "mission objectives" in flight simulator practice, airplane design, navigation, knowledge of aviation and aviation history, and crew cooperation.

Throughout the year, team members work on designing and building their own balsa gliders, learning about aviation weather and history, learning how to plan and navigate an actual airplane flight, and practicing how to fly such a flight on Microsoft FlightSim 2000 software. Teams also have the challenge of writing and performing a 3-5 minute play that manages to convey accurate information on the flight characteristics and history of an airplane they choose from a local air museum or at the local airport. A team scrapbook of their efforts will also be judged at regional and national competitions.

Regional competitions are held in the spring at air museums around the country. Winners of regional competitions are then brought to the EAA's annual AirVenture fly-in to compete on a national level, at the EAA's expense.

A non-competitive version of the program is also available for teachers who wish to include some of the Wild Blue Wonders activities into their classroom curriculum.

Want to test your aviation knowledge, experiment with some of these wild airplane designs, and maybe earn a trip to the EAA's AirVenture Fly-In? Wild Blue Wonders might just give you the wings you need to get your dreams off the ground!

For more information, contact:

Wild Blue Wonders
Experimental Aircraft Association
Phone: 920-426-4800
Email: education@eaa.org
Website: www.wildbluewonders.org

GLOSSARY OF TERMS

Ailerons – moveable surfaces on the back edges of an airplane's wing that can be moved up or down to make the airplane roll one way or another.

Airspeed Indicator – an instrument that tells the pilot how fast the plane is going.

Altimeter – an instrument that tells a pilot how high above sea level the plane is flying.

Amphibious Aircraft – aircraft that can land either in the water or on land.

Angle of Attack – the angle between an airplane's wing and its flight path. (The plane's flight path can be straight ahead, if the plane is flying level, pointing down if the plane is descending, or pointing up if the plane is climbing.)

Area Rule – an important factor in designing supersonic airplanes. An engineer named Richard Whitcomb figured out that a plane would go through the speed of sound more easily if it had less of a sharp jump in frontal *area* from its narrow nose to where the wings attached to the plane. Designers can reduce the big jump in area where the wings attach to a plane by narrowing the fuselage where the wings are or widening the fuselage just ahead of the wing.

Aspect Ratio – an aeronautical term that means the length of an airplane wing versus its width, front to back. A "high" aspect ratio wing is long and narrow. A "low" aspect ratio wing is short and wide.

Attitude Indicator – sometimes called an "artificial horizon," this is an instrument that tells a pilot the position of the airplane in relation to the true horizon. It will tell a pilot whether the airplane is level, climbing, descending, or turning.

Axis (or axes, plural) – an aeronautical term that refers to the way an airplane moves. If an airplane is moving its nose up and down, it's said to be "pitching" up and down along the longitudinal (lengthwise) "axis" of the plane.

Balanced Controls – special flight controls (usually ailerons and elevators) that are used on aerobatic planes. The hinge points of this kind of control surface are back from the front edge a little bit. This helps make the control surface more balanced and easier to move.

Bernoulli's Principle – a law of physics that states: The pressure in a fluid decreases as the speed of the fluid increases. The curve in an airplane wing speeds up the air going across it, which decreases the pressure above the wing. Since objects move toward areas of lower pressure, the wing moves up. This "lift" is what allows an airplane to fly.

Biplane – a plane that has two main wings, usually one above the other.

Canard – a surface forward of the plane's center of gravity that creates lift. Usually canards are located at the front of an airplane.

Center of Gravity – the point in an airplane where the plane would balance perfectly if suspended on the tip of a pole. This is also the point around which the airplane rotates when it pitches up or down, rolls right or left, or turns its nose left or right.

Center of Lift – the point on an airplane's wing where it is creating the most lift.

Compass – a basic navigation instrument that tells a pilot what the magnetic heading of the airplane is. A compass is oriented to the magnetic north pole, which is different from the true north pole, so the magnetic heading of an airplane can be slightly different from the true heading. But most navigation instruments and aids relate to magnetic headings.

Composite – something made of two or more different materials. In airplane design, one common type of "composite" structure is a "sandwich" with foam or honeycomb-structure material in between two layers of fiberglass.

Control Surfaces – moveable parts of an airplane that make it able to maneuver in the sky. The most common control surfaces are ailerons, rudders, and elevators.

Crankshaft – the part of a piston engine that turns the propeller. The firing of the pistons turns the crankshaft, which is attached to the propeller.

Density Altitude – the altitude of a plane or airport, adjusted for heat and humidity. (A 2,000 foot altitude airport will act like it is much higher on a hot, humid day. This means airplanes will need more runway distance to take off and land.)

Dihedral – the upward angle of an airplane's wings above a perfectly horizontal position. Most airplane wings, if looked at from the nose of the airplane, form a slight upward "v" shape. This helps make the plane more stable.

Directional Stability – the ability of an airplane to keep its nose pointed straight ahead or in a certain "direction." On an airplane, the vertical tail is the most important element in keeping the airplane's nose from swinging, or "yawing," left or right. So the vertical tail gives the airplane "directional stability."

Dope – a type of butyrate nitrate paint/filler that was used to make old cotton fabric airplane wing coverings stiff and strong.

Drag – anything that slows or disrupts the airflow over an airplane, slowing the plane down by countering the forward force of its engine "thrust."

Drag Chute – A parachute-type device that comes out from behind some very fast airplanes after they land to create more "drag" and help slow them down. The Space Shuttle also now uses a drag chute.

Drooped Ailerons – a type of aileron that helps a plane fly well at slow speeds. A drooped aileron will slide back and down when the plane's flaps are put down, so it helps create lift. From there, it still acts as a normal aileron, moving up and down to help the airplane turn.

Drooped leading edges – a kind of wing design to help planes fly better at slow speeds. The leading edge of these wings is angled down so it's easier for air to keep flowing over it, even when the plane is at a high angle of attack.

Electronic Flight Displays – Computer screen-type displays that some modern planes use to show a combination of engine, navigation, and flight information. Before the invention of computer, all this information was presented in individual dials and gauges.

Elevator – the flight control surface that pitches the tail of the airplane up or down. This allows the airplane to climb and descend.

Elevons – a type of flight control that acts as both an ELEVator (which pitches the plane up or down)and an and ailerON (which rolls the airplane right or left). These "dual-purpose" controls are called elevons.

Flaps – moveable surfaces on the inner trailing edge of an airplane's wing that can be extended downward to help the plane fly and land at slower speeds.

Floats – a type of landing gear that can be attached to a plane to allow it to land on water. Floats are long, slender, and filled with air, much like the pontoons on a pontoon boat.

Flying Boat – an airplane with a fuselage bottom shaped like the keel of a boat. This allows the plane to land in the water. Floatplanes can also land in water, but they have floats underneath the fuselage where the landing gear of conventional planes would be. Flying boats also have pontoons under the wings, to keep the wings from dipping in the water. They can generally land in rougher water than a floatplane. The old Pan Am Clipper airliners were flying boats.

Fowler Flaps – a type of flap that first extends backward on tracks to increase the wing area before dropping down. This helps the wing create more lift as the flaps are extended, which helps the plane fly better at slow speeds.

Frontal Area — the amount of the plane that would touch the surface of the water at any given point if you lowered a plane nose-first into a lake.

G Force – a force that is exerted on a plane and its pilot due to acceleration. One "G" is equal to one times the force of normal gravity on a body at rest. Three "Gs" is a force equal to three times the force of gravity on a body at rest. At three Gs, a piece of equipment that normally weighs one pound will exert the force of something weighing three pounds.

High Alpha – an aeronautical term meaning "high angle of attack."

HUD – Heads Up Display. This device puts the basic flight and navigation information up on a glass plate in front of the plane's front windscreen. This lets the pilot keep track of the plane's speed, altitude and direction without looking down in the cockpit. HUDs are used in many military fighters.

Hypersonic – speeds higher than five times the speed of sound (about 3,500 miles an hour)

Induced Drag – drag that is created by the movement of the airplane through the air. In the process of creating lift, air is disturbed. This disturbed air slows the airplane's movement somewhat and is known as "induced drag."

Laminar Flow – a perfectly streamlined flow of air along a solid boundary. A laminar flow wing is one that allows for the smoothest possible flow of air over the wing.

Lateral Stability – this refers to whether or not an airplane will want to return to level flight if you bump one wing up or down. If an airplane has good lateral stability, it means the wings really want to stay level.

Lift – an upward force created by the effect of air flowing over and under an airplane's wing.

Longitudinal Stability – the stability of an airplane in pitch. If a plane has good longitudinal stability, it will want to return to level flight after you pitch its nose up or down.

Monoplane – a plane with a single wing. Most modern planes are "monoplanes."

Multi-Function Displays – cathode ray tube (CRT) displays (computer screen-type displays) that a pilot can use to show several different types of information. Military planes often have multi-function displays in their cockpits.

NACA – the National Advisory Committee for Aeronautics. This organization was formed in 1915 to help solve problems of flight. It was incorporated into NASA once the space age began.

NASA – the National Aeronautics and Space Administration. This is the national agency whose job it is to oversee the exploration of space. It also conducts research to improve aircraft and spacecraft technology.

Negative Lift – when the design of an airfoil actually pulls that part of the airplane down toward the ground. Horizontal tails on airplanes produce "negative lift."

Neutral Stability – if an airplane has "neutral stability," it will not tend to return to level flight after the flight controls are disturbed. Rather, it will keep moving in whatever direction the controls were disturbed. So if a pilot pitched the plane up, the nose of the plane would continue to move upward, even if the pilot let go of the controls. This makes a plane more maneuverable — but more difficult to fly.

Newton's Third Law of Motion – the physics law that states: "For every action there is an equal and opposite reaction."

Nosewheel (Tricycle Gear) – an arrangement of landing gear that has two main gear under the middle part of the airplane and a third wheel at the nose of the plane, much like a tricyle's wheel arrangement.

Oblique Wing – an experimental wing design that allowed the wing to pivot around a center attach point on top of the plane's fuselage. The wing would stick out straight for take off and landing, and then pivot so one half of the wing was pointed forward and the other half trailed backward in cruise flight. The point of the design was to reduce the plane's drag in high-speed cruise flight.

Oxidizer – the substance that mixes with fuel to allow it to burn in an engine. In most airplane engines, air is the oxidizer. But rocket engines can't get air in space. So they carry another oxidizer, such as liquid oxygen, that they mix with their hydrogen fuel to allow it to burn.

Parafoil – a flexible, fabric wing that uses air to create a curved airfoil. Steerable parachutes and paragliders are parafoils. They have upper and lower surfaces with space in the middle that can fill with air. This creates a wing shape that creates lift and can be steered to a gentle landing.

Parasite Drag – drag created by the form or shape of airplane parts.

Piston Engine – an engine powered by pistons, or short cylinders moving up and down in a cylindrical casing. The force of these pistons moving up and down turns a crankshaft. In an airplane, the crankshaft is connected to the propeller, so the turning crankshaft that makes the propeller turn.

Pitch – movement of an airplane's nose up or down.

Positive Stability – an airplane that will tend to return to level flight after the flight controls have been disturbed.

Radial Engine – a piston engine whose cylinders are arranged in a circle behind the propeller. Many old biplanes and World War II airplanes had radial engines.

Ramjet – an engine that relies on an airplane's speed, rather than the turbine wheels of a conventional jet engine, to compress the air going into the combustion chamber. Ramjets are only effective at speeds faster than about 300 mph.

Reaction Controls – small rockets used to control spacecraft in space. The thrust from firing different reaction controls can move or turn spacecraft up, down, forward, backward, or sideways. The Space Shuttle uses 44 different reaction control rockets to keep it on course.

Rocket Engine – an engine that carries its own fuel and "air," or "oxidizer." The exhaust from the explosion of the fuel and "oxidizer" going out the back of the rocket moves the rocket forward.

Roll – movement of an airplane around the length of its fuselage. An airplane rolls by raising one wing and lowering the other.

Rudder – the flight control surface that turns the nose of the airplane left or right. In aeronautical terms, the rudder controls the "yaw" of the airplane.

Ruddervator – an unusual flight control surface that acts as both a RUDDER (which turns the nose of the airplane left or right) and and eleVATOR (which pitches the nose of the airplane up or down).

Scramjet – a Supersonic Combustion RAMJET. A scramjet works like a ramjet except that the air going into its combustion chamber is going faster than the speed of sound. A plane that flies eight times the speed of sound (around 5,600 miles an hour) might use a scramjet.

Slat – a device used to help a plane fly better at slow speeds. Slats extend forward and down from the leading edge of the wings to help keep air flowing over the wings even when they're pointed high in the air (at a high angle of attack).

Slot – another device to help planes fly better at slow speeds. Slots are long, thin gaps in the wing a little bit behind the leading edge. If the wing is pointed too high up in the air for air to flow over the leading edge, it can still flow through the slot and over the rest of the wing. This allows the wing to keep making lift.

Slotted Flaps – a kind of flap that allows air to flow in between the back of the wing and the top of the flap. This helps the flap create lift even at very slow speeds.

Sonic Boom – the noise caused by the shock wave that's created by an airplane flying at or faster than the speed of sound.

Spades – devices used on the control surfaces of aerobatic planes to make the controls easier to move, even when the plane is pulling tight maneuvers.

Speed Brakes – surfaces that can extend from an airplane to create extra drag and help slow it down in flight or just after landing.

Split Flaps – a device used on flying wing airplane designs to help the airplane turn or slow down. The flaps on the outside edges of the wing can "split" open, extending one part above the wing and one part below the wing. If the flap on only one wing is opened, it will create drag and help turn the airplane in that direction. If both are opened at the same time, the split flaps act as speed brakes to help the plane descend.

Spoilers – flap-type surfaces on the top of an airplane's wing that will "spoil" the air flow over the wing. This reduces the wing's lift and helps the airplane descend more quickly.

Stabilator – a kind of horizontal tail surface of a plane that acts as both a horizontal STABILizer and an elevATOR. This kind of surface is also known as an "all-flying tail" and is used in supersonic airplane designs.

Stall – what happens when air cannot flow over a wing, so the wing stops producing lift. Generally this is a result of pulling the plane up into too steep an angle, exceeding the "critical angle of attack." If the nose of the plane is lowered, air will start flowing over the wing again.

Stratosphere – the more stable part of our atmosphere that begins at about seven miles (36,000 feet) above the Earth and extends to about 31 miles (160,000 feet) above the Earth.

STOL – Short Take Off and Landing. This term is used to describe both modifications for airplanes and airplanes themselves that can take off and land in short distances.

Supercharger – a device that is used to make air going into an engine more dense. Superchargers are engine-driven pumps that use fan wheels to compress incoming air before it mixes with the fuel. They help engines produce more power and are very useful for planes flying at high altitudes, where the air is thin.

Supercritical Wing – a special kind of airfoil, or wing, design, developed by NASA, that has low drag at speeds approaching the speed of sound. For this reason, most airliners use a supercritical wing design.

Supersonic – speeds faster than the speed of sound. The speed of sound differs depending on outside air conditions, but at sea level it's approximately 700 miles an hour.

Swept Wings – Wings whose leading edges angle backward from the wing root (near the fuselage). These wings are put on planes meant to fly fast.

Symmetrical Wings – wings that are curved on both their top and bottom surfaces. These wings produce less lift than conventional wings but are good for inverted aerobatics – flight upside down.

Tachometer – an instrument that tells a pilot how fast the engine's propeller is turning, in "revolutions per minute," or "RPM."

Taildragger (conventional gear) – a plane whose landing gear is arranged so that there are two main gear wheels under the main part of the plane/wing, and a third small wheel at the tail of the plane. These planes will have their noses sticking up in the air at an angle when they're sitting on the ground. They are sometimes referred to as "conventional gear" planes because when aviation began, all "conventional" planes had tailwheels. Today, most planes are built with the third wheel under the nose.

Tail Rotor – a set of rotor blades on the tail of a helicopter that direct air sideways to keep the helicopter from spinning around from the movement of the main rotor blades above the aircraft.

Thermal Thicket – a region of speed above Mach 2 (2 times the speed of sound, or about 1,400 miles an hour) where the heat caused by the friction of air molecules speeding past an airplane's fuselage and wings becomes the most difficult design problem to overcome.

Throttle – the lever or knob in the cockpit that allows a pilot to adjust how much power the engine is producing.

Thrust – a forward force that propels an airplane through the air. Usually, thrust is produced by an airplane's engine, which sends air backward and thus propels the airplane forward.

Thrust Reversers – devices that extend behind a jet's engines to "reverse" the direction of the thrust, sending it forward to help slow the airplane down. In a turboprop, this same thing is accomplished by changing the angle of its propeller blades to send the air forward.

Thrust Vectoring – using some system to change the direction, or "vector," of an engine's exhaust to help steer the airplane or spacecraft. Jetskis also use a very basic thrust vectoring system to turn in the water.

Troposphere – the part of our atmosphere that extends from the surface up to about 7 miles (36,000 feet). This is where most of our weather occurs and where most airplanes fly.

Tundra Tires – very large tires used on airplanes designed to land in rough areas. Because the tires are so big, they can roll more easily over small rocks or holes without getting stuck.

Turbocharger – like a supercharger, a turbocharger is a device used to make the air going into an engine more dense. But a turbocharger's fan wheels are turned by the exhaust of the engine instead of by the engine's crankshaft. This generally makes a turbocharger more efficient than a supercharger.

Turbofan engine – a turbine (jet) engine that takes some of the air going into the engine and propels it with a fan straight out the back of the engine. So while most of the air goes through the main part of the engine, mixes with fuel, and burns, some air goes around that section and goes straight out the back of the engine. This provides some extra "free" thrust, so these engines are a little more efficient than straight turbojet engines. Most airliners today use turbofan engines.

Turbojet engine – a conventional turbine, or jet, engine that uses a series of fan wheels to compress air going into a chamber where it mixes with fuel, burns, and is forced out the back of the engine to produce power, or thrust. Jet engines work well at high speeds and high altitudes, but they burn a lot of fuel. So they're not very efficient for low or slow airplane flight.

Turboprop engine – a turbine engine that's used to turn a propeller. The thrust from these engines comes not from the engine exhaust (like a jet engine), but from the air pushed backward by the propeller. These engines are more efficient (use less fuel) than straight jet engines. So many small commuter airliners, which fly slower and lower than the big jets, use "turboprop" engines.

Turn and Bank Indicator – an instrument that tells a pilot whether or not the plane is in a turn, and whether the correct amount of both aileron and rudder controls are being used in that turn.

Vortex/Vortices – swirling, disturbed air, most commonly referring to the swirling, disturbed air that comes off the wingtip of a plane in flight. Vortices swirl like a horizontal tornado and create a lot of drag. They also create very turbulent air, so they can be dangerous for any plane following too closely behind the plane making the vortices.

Wing Area – the total top surface area of a wing (the length of the wing times the width, or "chord" of the wing).

Wing Camber – the curve of an airfoil or wing.

Wing Fences – devices used to help keep air flowing back over a wing. They are vertical strips of metal that are attached on the top of the wing, perpendicular to the leading edge (pointing from the front of the wing to the back). The help funnel the air flow and keep it smooth, which helps the wing keep creating lift. They are used by Short Take Off and Landing airplanes as well as some other planes, including jets.

Winglets – vertical fins put at the tips of a plane's wings to break up the turbulent, tornado-type air that would otherwise spin off the wingtips. This turbulent air causes drag, so winglets make a plane's wing more efficient.

Wing Loading – the amount of weight each square foot of wing area has to lift. If a plane weighs 1,000 pounds and has a wing area of 100 square feet, then each square foot of wing has to lift 10 pounds. So the plane would have a "wing loading" of 10 pounds per square foot.

Wing Planform – the shape of a wing if looked at from directly above the airplane.

Wing Root – the part of the wing that attaches to the fuselage, or body, of the airplane.

Wing Warping – an unusual way of controlling an airplane's direction. Instead of having moveable control surfaces, a wing warping design actually bends (or "warps") each wing down or up slightly to make the airplane turn. The first airplane built by the Wright Brothers used wing warping for controL.

Yaw – movement of an airplane's nose (or tail) left or right.

GLOSSARY OF AIRPLANES

Ames-Dryden AD-1
Manufacturer: Ames Industrial Company
When Built: 1979
Comments: A research aircraft called an "oblique wing" design because its wing could pivot forward in flight to create less drag.

Beech Baron
Manufacturer: Beechcraft (now Raytheon Aircraft)
When Built: 1960 – present
Comments: Comfortable four to six-seat airplane powered by two piston engines. Some models have turbochargers. Maximum speed is about 239 mph.

Beech King Air
Manufacturer: Beechcraft (now Raytheon Aircraft)
When Built: 1970 - present
Comments: The King Air is a pressurized, 6-10 seat plane used mostly for business travel. It's powered by two turboprop engines and has a maximum cruising speed of about 250-320 miles per hour, depending on the model.

Beech Starship
Manufacturer: Raytheon Aircraft
When Built: First ones built in 1989
Comments: The prototype for the unusual-looking Starship was originally designed by Burt Rutan's Scaled Composites company (Rutan also designed the Voyager). It has a forward canard design and is powered by two turboprop engines.

Beech V-35 "V-Tail" Bonanza
Manufacturer: Beechcraft (now Raytheon Aircraft)
When Built: 1966 – 1990s
Comments: All Bonanzas are comfortable 4-6 seat airplanes that have a maximum speed of about 200 miles per hour. They are powered with single piston engine and have retractable gear. The most notable part of this type of Bonanza is its "V"-shaped tail, which has less drag than a more conventional shaped tail.

Bell 206 JetRanger/206L LongRanger Helicopter
Manufacturer: Bell Helicopter Company
When Built: 1962 – present
Comments: These all-purpose light helicopters are two of the busiest workhorses in the flying world. They are used to carry sling loads of trees and equipment, for business transportation, police and emergency work, and even to shoot motion pictures.

Bell V-22 Tilt-Rotor
Manufacturer: Bell-Boeing
When Built: 1989 – present
Comments: This "tilt-rotor" can take off like a helicopter and then "tilt" its propellers forward to fly like an airplane. It can then tilt the propellers back up again to land like a helicopter, or land on a runway like a plane. The propellers are driven by turboprop engines.

Bell X-1
Manufactuer: Bell Aircraft Company
When Built: 1946
Comments: The X-1 was a rocket-powered research airplane that was drop-launched from a specially modified B-29 bomber. The X-1 was the first airplane to go supersonic, which was known as "breaking the sound barrier."

Bell X-5
Manufacturer: Bell Aircraft Company
When Built: 1952
Comments: The X-5 was a research plane designed with a "swing wing" that could be swept further back in flight, once the plane was moving fast. The X-5 gave researchers a lot of good information that made the F-14 and F-111 swing-wing airplanes possible to build.

Boeing 737
Manufacturer: The Boeing Company
When Built: 1967 - present
Comments: This airliner was first built with turbojet engines. Some 737s still have small engines. But new models, and many older models now, have larger turbofan engines.

Boeing 747
Manufacturer: The Boeing Company
When Built: 1969 – present
Comments: For a long time, this was the biggest airliner anyone had ever built. It has four turbofan engines and can weigh more than half a million pounds at take off!

Boeing 747 Shuttle Carrier Aircraft (SCA)
Manufacturer: The Boeing Company
When Built: 1977
Comments: This special version of the Boeing 747 airliner was modified specifically to carry the Space Shuttle back and forth between California (where it used to land all the time) and Florida (where it launches). It has special attach points on its back and two extra rudders on the tips of its horizontal to help its pilots keep control of the plane with the bulky Shuttle on its back.

Boeing/NASA B-52 Mothership
Manufacturer: The Boeing Company
When Built: Built in 1955, modified by NASA in 1959 to carry research planes.
Comments: The B-52s were military bombers that first flew in 1954 and are still in use today. This particular B-52 was modified by NASA to launch the X-15 rocket research plane from a special pylon under its wing.. Since 1959, this "mothership" has carried many more experimental planes, including a model of the experimental X-38 space vehicle NASA is now researching.

C-17
Manufacturer: McDonnell Douglas Corporation (now part of The Boeing Company)
When Built: 1991 – present
Comments: The C-17 is the military's newest cargo plane. It's powered by 4 jet engines but it still lands and takes off in a very short distance. It can also carry unusual cargo like Keiko, the "Free Willy" whale!

C-130 Hercules
Manufacturer: Lockheed Company
When Built: First Built 1954
Comments: The C-130 is one of the most widely used military cargo planes. It is powered by four turboprop engines. It has a high wing, landing gear that retracts into special compartments beside the fuselage and a rear loading ramp to make its cargo area as big and easy to use as possible.

Centurion
Manufacturer: AeroVironment
When Built: 1998
Comments: A high-altitude research airplane, flown by remote control, that is solar powered so it can remain in flight for days at a time.

Cessna 150
Manufacturer: Cessna Aircraft Company
When Built: First built in 1957
Comments: The Cessna 150 is probably the most popular and well-known training airplane. You can see this plane at almost any airport in America. It has a single piston engine, fixed gear, straight wing, and two seats. It flies about 100 miles an hour.

Cessna 172
Manufacturer: Cessna Aircraft Company
When Built: 1956 – present
Comments: The Cessna 172 "Skyhawk" is probably the most popular all-around general aviation airplane. It has four seats and goes a little faster than the Cessna 150, so many pilots use them for leisure or business flying, but it is also used a lot for training new pilots.

Cessna 182
Manufacturer: Cessna Aircraft Company
When Built: First built in 1965
Comments: The Cessna 182 "Skylane" is the big brother to Cessna's 172 Skyhawk. Its main differences are a more powerful engine (230 horsepower) and a controllable-pitch propeller (meaning that the pitch, or angle, of the blades can be adjusted for better performance).

Cessna AgWagon
Manufacturer: Cessna Aircraft Company
When Built: First built in 1965
Comments: The Cessna AgWagon is a cropduster airplane. It can hold 280 gallons of fertilizer, insecticide or chemicals, and has special corrosion proofing to keep the chemicals from damaging the plane. It also had a beefy cockpit structure and spring steel landing gear Cessna called "Land-O-Matic" gear because it was supposed to make the plane so easy to land.

Cessna Caravan
Manufacturer: Cessna Aircraft Company
When Built: 1982 – present
Comments: The Model 208 Caravan is a 10-14 seat airplane with one turboprop engine and fixed gear. They are used widely as cargo planes to get overnight delivery packages from small airports to big airports.

Cessna Citation X
Manufactuer: Cessna Aircraft Company
When Built: 1996 - present
Comments: The Citation X is one of the fastest business jets that Cessna builds. It is powered by two turbojet engines and can fly Mach .98 – almost the speed of sound.

Christen Eagle
Manufacturer: Kitplane built by individual pilots
When built: First built in 1977
Comments: The Christen Eagle was designed specifically to do sport aerobatics. It's strong and very maneuverable.

Convair F-102/F-102A
Manufacturer: Convair division of General Dynamics
When Built: 1953
Comments: The F-102 was supposed to go supersonic (faster than the speed of sound) in level flight. But it wasn't doing well in flight tests. Then a NASA engineer figured out that if they made the fuselage narrower at the point where the wings joined the body, it would go faster. So the plane was redesigned and the new, faster plane was called the F-102A. Its maximum speed was about 825 miles an hour, or about Mach 1.25.

Douglas D-558-2 Skyrocket
Manufacturer: Douglas Aircraft Company
When Built: 1948
Comments: The Skyrocket was a rocket-powered research plane used to explore flight at and above the speed of sound. It was the first plane to go Mach 2, or two times the speed of sound.

Douglas X-3
Manufacturer: Douglas Aircraft Company
When Built: 1954
Comments: The X-3 was supposed to test flight above Mach 2 with jet engines. It never flew that fast. But it still helped pilots learn some important things about controlling airplanes that fly faster than the speed of sound.

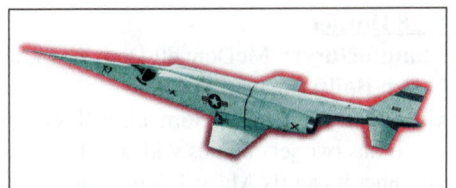

ER-2
Manufacturer: Lockheed Company
When Built: 1981
Comments: The jet-powered ER-2 is based on the design of a 1950s Lockheed spy plane called the U-2. The ER-2 has long, narrow wings, which helps it fly at high altitudes. This makes it a good plane for doing high-altitude atmospheric research for NASA.

Erickson Skycrane LLCS-64E
Manufacturer: Erickson Aircrane Company
When Built: First flown in 1968
Comments: The Skycrane helicopter is a cargo helicopter that is specially built for carrying very large sling loads (loads carried on a cable underneath the helicopter).

Extra 300S
Manufacturer: Designed by Walter Extra. Built by Extra Flugzeugbau GmbH.
When Built: 1992 - present
Comments: The Extra 300S is a high performance aerobatic plane with a very strong, smooth composite wing that can withstand 10 positive or negative "Gs" in aerobatic maneuvers. The plane can also cruise at almost 200 miles an hour and lands at only 60 miles an hour. Patty Wagstaff flies an Extra 300S in her air show routines.

F-111 Aardvark
Manufacturer: General Dynamics
When Built: First built in 1964
Comments: Swing-wing fighter/bomber in its military life, NASA used the F-111 to test a wing that could change how much curve it had in it while the airplane was in flight.

F-16 Falcon
Manufacturer: General Dynamics (now part of Lockheed Martin)
When Built: First built 1974
Comments: The F-16 was one of the first jet fighters to have computers helping to make it controllable. F-16s are still in wide use today in many military roles.

F-16XL
Manufacturer: General Dynamics
When Built: 1982
Comments: The F-16XL was a prototype of a new kind of F-16 that would have had a "cranked arrow" delta wing shape. General Dynamics decided not to build the airplane, but NASA used the airplane to test supersonic air flow.

F-18 Hornet
Manufacturer: McDonnell Douglas (now part of The Boeing Company)
When Built: First built in 1978
Comments: The F-18 Hornet is a Navy fighter that takes off and lands on aircraft carriers. It has two jet engines with afterburners and is a fly-by-wire (computer controlled) airplane. It can fly Mach 1.8, or almost 1,200 miles an hour.

F-104 Starfighter
Manufacturer: Lockheed Company
When Built: 1954 – 1979
Comments: The F-104 was one of the fastest jet fighters ever built. It could fly Mach 2.2, or about 1,450 miles an hour. It was nicknamed "A missile with a man in it" because it had such tiny wings and flew so fast.

Flying Wing (N9M-B)
Manufacturer: Northrop Corporation
When Built: 1944; rebuilt in 1994
Comments: This small N9M-B prototype flying wing is the last flyable version of a proposed bomber designed and built by the Northrop company in the 1940s. The decaying remains of the N9M-B were rebuilt by volunteers over 13 years, and the plane flew again in 1994.

Glider – Swift S-1
Manufacturer: Swift (Built in Poland)
When Built: 1991
Comments: This glider was built for aerobatic competition, so its wings aren't as long and narrow as some other gliders. But it still can glide 28 miles for every mile up in the air it is. Sailplanes (gliders) built for long-distance flying can glide up to 50 miles for every mile (5,280 feet) up in the air they are.

Gossamer Albatross
Manufacturer: Designed by Dr. Paul MacCready, built by Aerovironment, Inc.
When Built: 1979
Comments: The Gossamer Albatross was the big brother to the Gossamer Condor, which became the first plane to achieve human-powered flight in 1977. The Albatross weighed 70 pounds and had a wingspan of almost 94 feet. The pilot made the propeller spin by turning pedals with his feet.

Grumman Tiger
Manufacturer: Grumman American
When Built: First built in 1975
Comments: This sporty four-seat airplane goes about 150 miles an hour. Instead of doors, it has a canopy that can be slid back partway during flight. It also has a back seat that folds down for cargo space or to make a sleeping area overnight.

AV-8 Harrier
Manufacturer: McDonnell Douglas (now part of The Boeing Company)
When Built: First built by British Aerospace in 1969
Comments: This unusual attack jet can take off and land vertically by turning its engine exhaust to face directly toward the ground. It then rotates the exhaust backward to move the plane forward.

Hawker 800
Manufacturer: Raytheon Aircraft
When Built: First built in 1983. First Raytheon Hawker 800XP delivered in 1995.
Comments: The Hawker 800XP is a business jet that can carry 10-15 passengers and flies more than 500 mph.

HiMAT (Highly Maneuverable Aircraft Technology)
Manufacturer: Rockwell International
When Built: 1979
Comments: The HiMAT was a scale-model NASA research plane, flown by remote control. It was built to test ways to make planes more maneuverable.

Jetcruzer
Manufacturer: AASI Aircraft (Advanced Aerodynamics & Structures, Inc.)
When Built: First one built in 1998
Comments: The Jetcruzer is a business plane made of composite materials. It has a forward canard and a single turboprop "pusher" engine at the back. It flies at 360 miles an hour, but it also has drooped leading edges to help it fly better at slower speeds.

Lancair
Manufacturer: Individual pilots build these planes from kits
When Built: First Lancairs flew in the 1980s. New models are still being built.
Comments: The Lancair is a composite plane that is very sleek and has very smooth wings and surfaces. This means it has very little drag, so it flies very fast. Some Lancairs can fly 300 miles an hour.

Lifting Bodies
Manufacturer: Martin-Marietta (X-24A) and Northrop (M2-F3 and HL-10)
When Built: 1962-1970
Comments: All of these "lifting bodies" were research planes to test a possible design for a new spacecraft that could glide back to a normal landing on Earth. They were called "lifting bodies" because they had no wings. They got the "lift" they needed to fly from the curved shape of their fuselages (or "bodies").

Long EZ
Manufacturer: Designed by Burt Rutan, built by individual pilots from plans.
When Built: First ones built in the early 1980s. Many Long EZs are still being built.
Comments: The Long EZ (and the smaller Vari Eze) is a "homebuilt" plane that pilots can build in their garages or hangars. It has a forward canard instead of a horizontal tail at the back of the plane. It also has two small vertical tails with rudders at the tips of its wings instead of the one big vertical tail and rudder that more conventional planes have.

Lunar Landing Research/Training Vehicles (LLRV/LLTV)
Manufacturer: Bell Aerosystems Company
When Built: 1964
Comments: These "flying bedsteads" were built to figure out how to land on the moon. All the astronauts who landed the "lunar modules" on the moon practiced first in these.

Luscombe Model 8
Manufacturer: Luscombe Airplane Corporation/Silvaire Airplane Company
When Built: 1938-1942 and 1945 – 1959
Comments: The Luscombe Model 8 is a fun little taildragger (meaning it has its 3rd wheel at its tail, not under its nose) that goes about 100 miles an hour. Many are still flying today.

MD-11 Airliner
Manufacturer: McDonnell Douglas (now part of The Boeing Company)
When Built: 1989 – present
Comments: The MD-11 is one of the newest airliners flying today. It is a fly-by-wire design. This means that the control surfaces are linked electronically (not with mechanical cables) to the pilot's control yoke with the help of a computer.

Nemesis racer (Sharp Nemesis DR-90)
Manufacturer: Jon Sharp (experimental plane built by individual pilots)
When Built: 1990
Comments: The little Nemesis racer is a very sleek, fast, efficient design. It can fly 300 miles an hour. And even though all the planes in its racing class have to use the same engine, the Nemesis was not beaten in a race from 1991 until it was retired in 2000.

NOTAR Helicopter (MD Explorer)
Manufacturer: MD Helicopter Company
When Built: 1994-present
Comments: The NOTAR design (which stands for NO TAil Rotor) is used on several MD Helicopters. Instead of tail rotor blades, the NOTAR uses exhaust air to keep the tail of the helicopter steady. This NOTAR helicopter is an MD Explorer, a twin-engine, turbine-engine powered helicopter.

Oracle Turbo Raven
Manufacturer: Built by Composites, Unlimited; based on the AcroTech G-202
When Built: 1998
Comments: The Oracle Turbo Raven was an extremely manueverable turboprop-powered aerobatic plane designed and built for air show performer Wayne Handley. It weighed only 1,600 pounds empty, so its engine put out more pounds of thrust than the airplane weighed. This meant it could fly straight up in the air!

P-51 Mustang
Manufacturer: North American Aviation
When Built: 1941 - 1945
Comments: The P-51 Mustang is probably the most classic fighter of World War II. It had a V-12 (12-cylinder) engine made by Rolls Royce

Pathfinder
Manufacturer: AeroVironment
When Built: 1993
Comments: A high-altitude, solar-powered research airplane designed to stay aloft for long periods of time. Very similar to the Centurion, but smaller: the Pathfinder's wingspan is 120 feet long, and the Centurion's wingspan is 206 feet long. Flown by remote control.

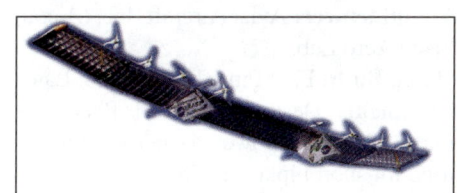

Paraglider
Manufacturer: Paragliding canopies are made by a number of different companies (For more information, contact the U.S. Hang Gliding Association in Colorado Springs, CO)
When Built: First ones built in the late 1980s
Comments: Paragliders are flexible airfoils that fill with air in flight to create a stable "wing" above the pilot. They can be launched by running down a steep hillside.

Paresev
Manufacturer: Engineers at the Dryden Flight Research Center
When Built: 1962
Comments: The "Paraglider Research Vehicle," or "Paresev" was a research plane built to help test whether an inflatable wing could be used to bring the early space capsules back to an Earth landing.

Perseus
Manufacturer: Aurora Flight Sciences Corp.
When Built: First prototype built in 1991. Perseus A model built in 1993.
Comments: A research aircraft designed for long-range, high-altitude flight. Carried liquid oxygen to mix with the fuel to make the engine able to operate well in the the very thin air (few air molecules) at high altitude.

Pilatus PC-6 Porter
Manufacturer: Pilatus Aircraft (Switzerland)
When Built: 1959 – present
Comments: The boxy Pilatus Porter is an excellent short take off and landing airplane. It has a turboprop engine and is used for carrying cargo into remote places as well as jobs like carrying skydivers.

Piper J-3 Cub
Manufacturer: Piper Aircraft Corporation
When Built: First built in 1936
Comments: The Piper J-3 Cub is one of the most classic airplanes of all time. It has fabric-covered wings and a door that folds open in flight, making it a fun airplane for low, slow sightseeing.

Piper PA-18 Super Cub
Manufacturer: Piper Aircraft Corporation
When Built: 1949-1978
Comments: The Super Cub is an even better short field airplane than its little brother, the classic Piper Cub, because it has big flaps and a bigger engine. It can carry more, as well.

Pitts Biplane
Manufacturer: Aviat Aircraft, Inc. (A couple of models are also sold as kitplanes by Steen Aero Lab.)
When Built: First Pitts flew in 1944. Later versions still manufactured today.
Comments: Designed by Curtis Pitts in 1944 as a sport plane, the Pitts biplane evolved into a 200+ horsepower, 4-aileron, high performance aerobatic airplane. Some are also used for sport biplane racing.

Space Shuttle
Manufacturer: North American-Rockwell
When Built: First orbiter built in 1977
Comments: The Space Shuttle uses internal rocket engines and external rocket boosters to get into space. Its wings then allow it to glide back to a runway landing on Earth.

R-44 Raven
Manufacturer: Robinson Helicopter Company
When Built: 1993 – present
Comments: The R-44 is one of the best-selling helicopters in the world. It has four seats and is powered by a piston engine, so it is less expensive than comparable turbine-engine helicopters, but it can still cruise at 130 mph.

Rutan Boomerang
Manufacturer: Scaled Composites, Inc.
When Built: Prototype, built in 1998
Comments: The Boomerang's lopsided design is an attempt to keep both engines close to the center, which is safer if one of the engines has a problem.

Sherpa
Manufacturer: Sherpa Aircraft
When Built: First one built in 1993
Comments: The Sherpa was designed as a STOL airplane. It was powered by a 400 horsepower engine and was originally designed to hold five people. A couple of different versions of the plane are now being developed as kits that pilots can build themselves.

SR-71 Blackbird
Manufacturer: Lockheed Company
When Built: First built in 1963
Comments: The titanium SR-71 is the fastest jet-powered airplane known to exist in the world. It flies more than 3 times the speed of sound (Mach 3), or about 2,000 miles an hour. It also flies more than 80,000 feet (16 miles!) up in the air.

Taylorcraft
Manufacturer: Taylorcraft Aviation Corporation/Taylorcraft Incorporated
When Built: 1946–1958
Comments: Taylorcrafts are simple, two-seat tailwheel airplanes that fly 90-100 miles an hour. There are still many of them flying today.

Tupolev Tu-144 SST
Manufacturer: Tupolev (Russian)
When Built: First built in 1968
Comments: The Tu-144 was the first supersonic transport ever built (its first flight was about two months before the BAC Concorde). It could fly as fast as Mach 2.35 (more than two times the speed of sound). Only 13 were ever built.

Ultralights
Manufacturer: Numerous manufacturers
When Built: 1970s - present
Comments: Ultralights vary from motorized hang gliders to composite-structure fuselage and wing designs. But they all are extremely lightweight, with very small engines. They are not certified as standard category aircraft, and pilots do not have to have a pilot's license from the Federal Aviation Administration (FAA) to fly them.

Voyager
Manufacturer: Designed by Burt Rutan, built by volunteers
When Built: 1986
Comments: The Voyager, flown by pilots Dick Rutan and Jeanna Yeager, was the first airplane to fly around the world non-stop, without taking on any additional fuel.

X-15
Manufacturer: North American Aviation
When Built: Three planes built, 1959-1961
Comments: The rocket-powered X-15 was the first plane to fly in "space," and it is still the fastest plane that has ever flown. It flew almost seven times the speed of sound, or over 4,000 miles an hour.

X-29
Manufacturer: Grumman Corporation
When Built: Only two built; first one flew in 1984, the second first flew in 1989.
Comments: The X-29 was a NASA/US Air Force research plane designed to explore computerized aircraft controls, and the possible advantages of a forward swept wing design.

X-31
Manufacturer: Rockwell/Deutsche Aerospace
When Built: Two airplanes built, the first in 1990, the second in 1991.
Comments: The X-31 was a research airplane built to test how thrust-vectoring (angling the jet engine exhaust) could make a fighter plane more maneuverable.

X-36
Manufacturer: McDonnell Douglas (now part of The Boeing Company)
When Built: 1997
Comments: The X-36 is a remote-control research plane. It's helping engineers learn about designing "tail-less" airplanes.

X-38
Manufacturer: Scaled Composites, Inc.
When Built: 1997
Comments: This is a scale model of a new type of spacecraft that might be able to bring astronauts back from the space station in an emergency. It would fly back down to about 20,000 feet, and then land under a steerable parachute.

X-43 (Hyper X)
Manufacturer: MicroCraft, Inc.
When Built: 1999
Comments: The X-43 is a scale model research plane that will be launched on the front of a small rocket. It will go "hypersonic," or between seven and 10 times the speed of sound. Engineers are building it to learn more about how to build a scramjet engine.

Zenair CH-701
Manufacturer: Zenair Aircraft
When Built: 1986 – present
Comments: The Zenair CH-701 is a small, two-place kitplane that individual pilots can build from parts supplied by the Zenair Aircraft Company. It's a good plane for landing on short runways.

AVIATION/AEROSPACE RESOURCE GUIDE

The following is a list of just some of the resources and organizations that can help you get more involved in flying, designing, or learning more about airplanes.

Academy of Model Aeronautics
(a national model airplane association)
www.modelaircraft.org

Aircraft Owners and Pilots Association (AOPA)
421 Aviation Way
Frederick, MD 20701
1-800-USA-AOPA
www.aopa.org
AOPA has a "Project Pilot" program to help mentor people who want to learn to fly. The organization has many other resources, as well.

Aviation Explorer Scouts
To find out more about local explorer scout/aviation explorer scout troops, call your local Boys Scouts of America service center (listed in the phone book).
Or contact the Explorer Scouts web site:
www.learning-for-life.org
(Click on "aviation exploring," then type in your city and state and it will tell you where the closest troop is)

Aviation Scholarship Foundation
Chicago, IL
708-448-1914
http://members.aol.com/kids/fly/
The Aviation Scholarship Foundation is an organization that helps low-income teenagers from the south Chicago area get glider and airplane licenses.

Experimental Aircraft Association (EAA)
3000 Poberezny Rd
P.O. Box 3065
Oshkosh, WI 54901
Phone: 920-426-4800
Website: www.eaa.org
The EAA has over 1,000 chapters located around the country and also has a number of programs oriented toward getting young people involved in aviation. A few of these programs are:

EAA Aviation Foundation Young Eagles Program
Phone: 920-426-4800
Email: yeagles@eaa.org
Website: www.youngeagles.org
The EAA Young Eagles program matches volunteer pilots who want to share their love of flight with young people who would like an airplane ride to see what flight is like.

EAA Aviation Foundation's Air Academy
Phone: 920-426-4800
Email: education@eaa.org
Website: www.eaa.org/education/youth_programs.html
The Air Academy is a series of week-long summer residence programs at EAA headquarters in Oshkosh, Wisconsin, for young people ages 12-18. In addition to a wide variety of recreational activities, participants get to learn more about flight through activities such as designing and building their own gliders, hot air balloons and rockets, helping to build wing ribs, working with flight simulators, and even get actual airplane flights (if weather conditions permit).

AirVenture/KidVenture
Phone: 920-426-4800
Email: convention@eaa.org
Website: www.eaa.org
During the last week of July every year, the EAA hosts AirVenture – the largest fly-in in the world. More than 12,000 airplanes and 750,000 people from around the world gather in Oshkosh, Wisconsin for a week of fun flying and aviation activities. As part of the fly-in, the EAA also offers young people a daily KidVenture program, which gives young people hands-on opportunities to learn more about flight and airplane design.

NATIONAL AERONAUTICS AND SPACE ADMINISTRATION (NASA)

NASA has many different resources for anyone looking for more information on aircraft and spacecraft research and design. These include:

NASA Education Home Page
http://education.nasa.gov

NASA Aeronautics Centers' Education Homepages:

NASA Ames Research Center –
http://george.arc.nasa.gov/dx/basket/storiesetc/Edprogsa.html

NASA Dryden Flight Research Center –
http://dfrc.nasa.gov/trc

NASA Langley Research Center –
http://edu.larc.nasa.gov

NASA Glenn Research Center –
http://www.grc.nasa.gov/Doc/educatn.htm

NASA Aeronautics Photographs and Images:
http://nix.nasa.gov

NASA's Learning Technologies Project
http://learn.lvv.nasa.gov
This web page gives information on a variety of Internet projects that teachers and students can use to explore NASA resources and learn about NASA missions.

NASA Student Involvement Program (NSIP)
www.NSIP.net
This web page gives information on design competitions and learning activities students can undertake to explore space and Earth.

NASA Educator Resource Center Network
http://spacelink.nasa.gov/Educational.Services/Educational Services/How.to.Access.Information/
Educator.Resource.Center.Network.-.ERCN/.index.html
These centers disseminate information on NASA programs, technologies, and discoveries free to educators.

NASA Office of Aero-Space Technology
http://www.hq.nasa.gov/office/aero
This is the web page for NASA's Washington, D.C. office for aeronautics.

Get-Away Special (GAS can) and Space Experiment Module (SEM)
Space Shuttle experiments
For more information on this program, contact:
NASA Goddard Space Flight Center
Mail Code 870
Beltsville, MD 20771
(301) 286-6760
http://sspp.gsfc.nasa.gov/sem/sem.html
http://sspp.gsfc.nasa.gov/gas/gas.html

Soaring Society of America
P.O. Box E
Hobbs, NM 88241
(505) 392-1177

University of North Dakota International Aerospace Camp
UND Aerospace
University of North Dakota
Box 9007
Grand Forks, ND 58202
1-800-258-1525
www.aero.und.edu
The University of North Dakota sponsors summer aerospace camps for teenagers.

United States Ultralight Association (USUA)
301-695-9100
www.usua.com
www.ultralightflying.com

United States Hang Gliding Association
Colorado Springs, CO
1-719-632-8300
www.ushga.org

U.S. Space Camp
P.O. Box 070015
Huntsville, AL 35807
Space Camp:1-800-637-7223

Aviation Challenge Camp: 1-800-533-7281
www.spacecamp.com

The U.S. Space Camp organization offers week-long space camps for kids in grades 4-12 in three locations: Huntsville, AL; Titusville, FL; and Mountain View, CA. It also offers more airplane-oriented "Aviation Challenge" camps for grades 4-12 in Huntsville, AL and Atwater, CA.

Women In Aviation, International
(An organization dedicated to supporting women in aviation careers)
www.wiai.org

ACKNOWLEDGEMENTS

This book started out as a bright idea by a NASA manager who remembered having a hard time finding books that explained flight and planes well when he was young. It was a great idea, but turning that idea into reality took a lot of assistance, dedication, effort, and patience from a lot of very talented people.

A writer can only do so much, especially in a book where graphics and graphic design play such an important role. Kimberly Sanders, who is a talented flight instructor and pilot as well as a gifted artist and graphic designer, created the design for the book. Her creativity and enthusiastic love of flight are evident on every page. Turning that design into reality took another, equally talented effort by the NASA graphic design team of Dennis Calaba, David Faust and Steve Lighthill, who took Kimberly's drawings gave them color, life, and the refinement of a beautiful, camera-ready-art product – under an extremely tight deadline.

But this book could not have been published without the support and perseverance of others, as well. Jenny Baer-Riedhart, chief of Public Affairs, Commercialization and Education at NASA's Dryden Flight Research Center, revived the project after it had sat dormant for over a year and a half, waiting for a publisher. Then Tom Poberezny threw the support of the Experimental Aircraft Association (EAA) behind it, and we finally had the critical mass we needed to bring *Wild Blue Wonders* to life.

The book was still far from finished, however. We would have had nothing to publish if it weren't for the many individuals and companies who cheerfully and quickly sent photos and helped me track down odd aircraft information and graphics. Why did so many people pitch in and cooperate? Well, we did try to ask nicely. But I think it also was because those of us whose lives have been made so much richer by flying or designing airplanes want to help sustain that all-important life spark of imagination in the eyes of young people who are still wise enough to know that dreams are possible. We hope, in our heart of hearts, that this book helps to do that.

The first measure of gratitude has to go to everyone at NASA's Dryden Flight Research Center and the EAA who made this project possible, of course. But I also need to thank everyone who agreed to be a "Real-Life Profile" for the book, as well as the folks at Bell-Textron Helicopters, The Boeing Company, Cessna Aircraft Company, Cirrus Aircraft, HAI, Roger Tonry of "Lost Squadron.com," MD Helicopters, Pilatus Aircraft, Raytheon Aircraft, Six Flags "Magic Mountain," Textron-Lycoming, The Air Museum "Planes of Fame," the U.S. Hang Gliding Association, Carey Gray, Jim Koepnick of the EAA photo department, Tony Landis and Carla Thomas of the NASA Dryden photo lab, and photographers Paul Bowen, Kurt Hoy, Thomas Hunziker, Forest Johnson, and Lani Muche for contributing or helping with photos for the book.

My thanks also to all the engineers at the Lockheed "Skunk Works" who worked with me on how to explain complicated aerodynamic laws without the use of formulas, John D. "Dill" Hunley, who contributed invaluable assistance to the project in the 11th hour, and to Celia Van der Pool for her expert educational evaluation of the book's content. And, finally, my thanks to both Dan Berger and Jim Dale for their help with the paper airplanes, which they learned to make and draw back when they, too, were wise enough to know that anything … including flight … was possible.

Lane Wallace
Santa Rosa, CA
June 1, 2001

About the Author

Lane Wallace, a regular columnist and the West Coast Editor for FLYING Magazine, is a nationally-known and respected aerospace writer and author. She learned to fly in 1986 after being inspired by a biplane flying by overhead, and her love affair with airplanes continues to this day. She owned a 1946 Cessna 120 for seven years and now owns a 1977 Grumman Cheetah.

In addition to her work at FLYING, Ms. Wallace has written three illustrated history books for NASA on the agency's efforts and accomplishments in aeronautics and space research. She also wrote and co-produced a three-part documentary series on the human adventure of flight research called "Test Flights: Beyond the Limits" that aired on The Learning Channel in August 1999.

Along the way, Ms. Wallace's work has earned her numerous citations and awards, including an honorary membership in the Air Force Society of Wild Weasels, a citation for Outstanding Contributions to Preserve General Aviation from the Torrance, California Airport Association, and a 1994 Washington Edpress Silver Award for Excellence in Print.

Photo by Scott Bogunia

About the Experimental Aircraft Association

The Experimental Aircraft Association is a not-for-profit organization founded in 1953 with the mission of making aviation accessible to all who wish to participate while maintaining high standards of quality and safety. It currently has over 170,000 members and more than 1,000 local chapters around the country. Those chapters sponsor numerous activities and events, including aircraft design and building workshops, fly-ins, airport days, and other community and educational events. In addition, the EAA's annual EAA AirVenture gathering in Oshkosh is known as one of the world's largest and most significant aviation events. The EAA also publishes several aviation-oriented magazines and maintains an expansive aviation museum and gift shop at its Wisconsin headquarters that attracts over 150,000 visitors a year.

About The EAA Aviation Foundation

In 1962, the EAA established the EAA Aviation Foundation, dedicated to the education, history, and development of sport aviation. One of the Foundation's most important efforts is the Young Eagles Program, created to give a flight experience to young people. The Foundation and EAA volunteer pilots plan to give one million young people a demonstration airplane ride by December 17, 2003 – the 100th anniversary of powered flight and the EAA's 50th anniversary year.

The Foundation also administers an extensive scholarship program for young people interested in aviation-related careers. In addition, it coordinates a number of youth and adult aviation education programs that utilize the adventure of aviation to motivate students to pursue science, math, and technology-related careers.

About NASA and the Dryden Flight Research Center

The National Aeronautics and Space Administration (NASA) was created in 1958 to advance aeronautics and space technology and to both advance and communicate scientific knowledge and understanding of the Earth, the solar system, and the universe. NASA evolved from the National Advisory Committee for Aeronautics, which was formed in 1915 to help solve the problems of flight, and one of NASA's main missions continues to be the research and testing of new ideas in aircraft, engine and control system design and technology. The Dryden Flight Research Center, located on Edwards Air Force Base in Edwards, California, is the NASA center where many of those ideas actually take flight.

Since its creation, NASA also has had a substantial commitment to education with the goal of inspiring America's students, creating learning opportunities and enlightening inquisitive minds. Recognizing that aviation and spaceflight can serve as powerful tools for teaching science, math, and technology, NASA has developed a wide variety of educational programs and resources that draw on some of the lessons and excitement of exploring flight and space. These programs include teacher workshops, curriculum development, and a variety of school programs provided by local NASA Centers like Dryden. NASA provides additional educational material through a nationwide network of educator resource centers, CD-ROMs, the internet, and other media, and even public television station programming. For young people wishing to get more involved in exploring flight and space, NASA offers a number of student programs such as the summer internship programs and a National Student Involvement Program (NSIP). Through programs like these, NASA hopes to turn today's students into tomorrow's explorers.

Glider Template (photocopy or trace, then cut out per instructions on page 30)

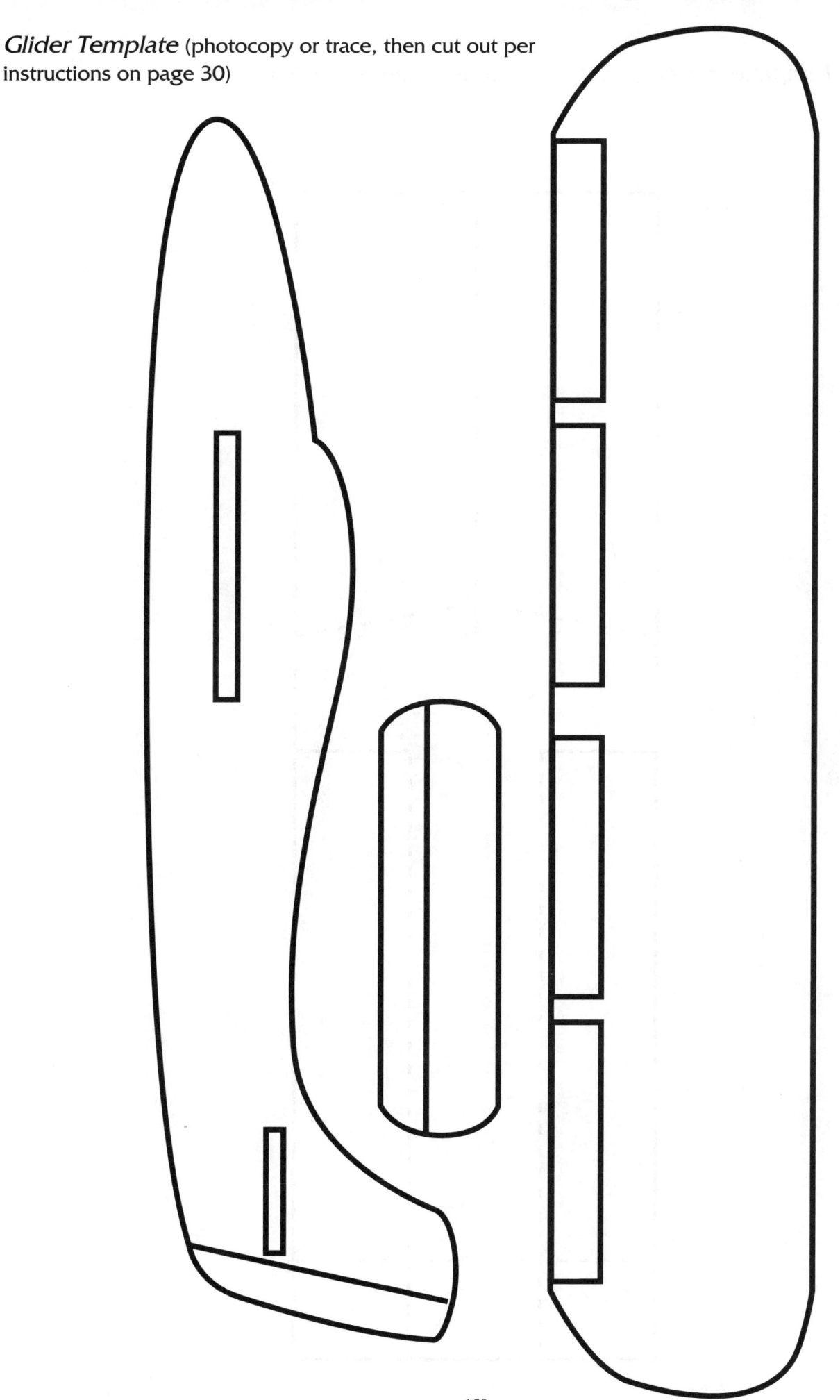

Helicopter Template (photocopy or trace, then cut out per instructions on page 71)

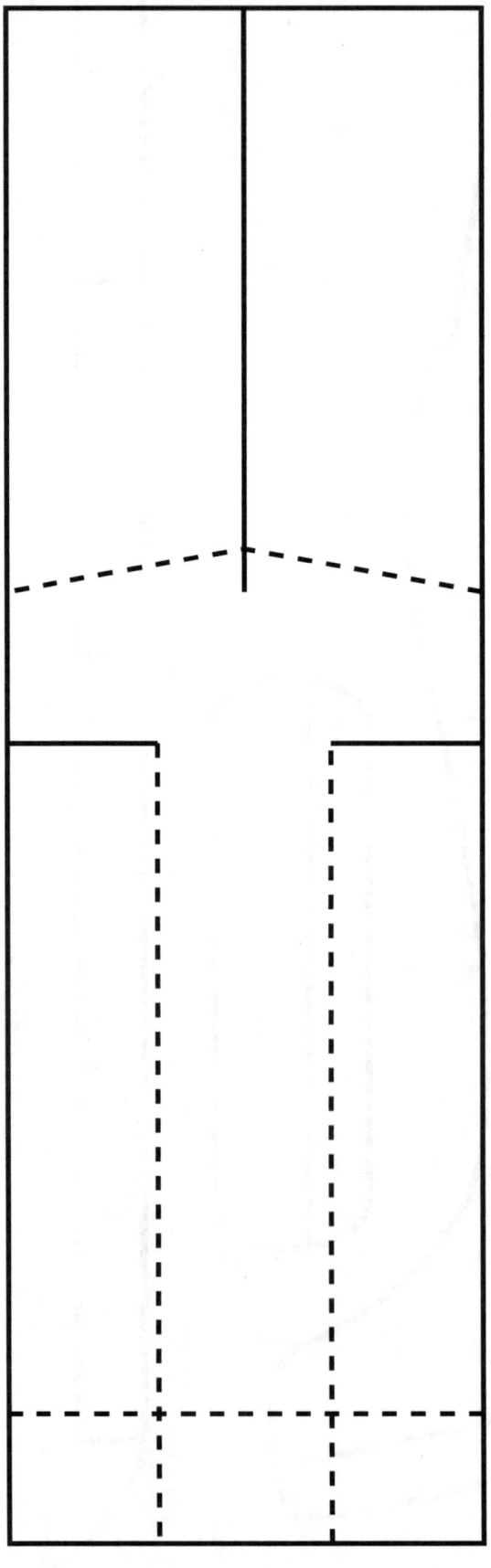